Not from Here

Selected UFO Articles: Volume One

Preston Dennett

Artwork by Christine Kesara Dennett

Blue Giant Books

Non-fiction
ISBN: 9780692650219
1.   Extraterrestrials, Aliens. 2. UFOs. 3. New Age. 4.
Paranormal, Supernatural, Metaphysical. 6. Science,
Astronomy. I. Title

Portions of this book have appeared in the following
publications: *Fate Magazine, Llewellyn Journal, the MUFON UFO
Journal, Perihelion, UFO Encounters, UFO Files, and UFO
Universe.*

Contents

Introduction

It all began one November evening in 1986. I was watching the news on TV and heard about one of those ridiculous UFO sightings. The pilot of a Japanese commercial airline claimed to have seen a UFO while flying over Alaska. The newscasters laughed nervously, joked about the incident and moved on to the next news item.

But in that instant my life changed forever. I thought to myself, this pilot is lying. Maybe he was suffering from "highway hypnosis" and hallucinated the object. Perhaps it was just a reflection off the ice-cap. I later learned that the object was larger than his plane and paced it for several miles. It appeared on the jet's onboard radar, and on ground radar, and was in view for nearly an hour.

None of these details were revealed on the news report about the incident, which interested me enough to mention it at the office where I worked. I soon got an incredible shock. The people that I had worked with for years began to tell me of their own UFO stories. One lady told me that she and her family saw a darting star-like object while camping in the San Bernardino Mountains of southern California. Another lady told me that she, her best friend and her mother were followed by a metallic disk with colored lights around the perimeter which hovered over their car as they drove home. It was strange, she said, because the drive which normally lasted five minutes took over an hour. Somehow they had lost time.

I then made the mistake of asking my friends and family. I learned that my brother and his two friends had seen a metallic object with colored lights and a dome shape on top in Reseda, California. My sister-in-law and her two friends observed three glowing objects over Van Nuys Air Force Reserve Base, in California. A close friend (and her friend) saw an egg-shaped object which emitted a low buzzing noise move overhead in Topanga, California. Another friend was with his girlfriend in Topanga Canyon when they saw a triangular formation of lights hovering in place low in the sky. The objects swooped at them, at which point they became disoriented and frightened and fled the area.

I continued to ask everyone I knew if they had ever encountered a UFO, and before long, I had an impressive collection of accounts. I was shocked. Could UFOs be real?

Determined to discover the truth, I went to the library to see if they had any books on the subject. I found a surprisingly wide variety. I quickly devoured them all--looking for the proof I hoped I would find--that UFOs can be explained as hoaxes, hallucinations or misperceptions.

Instead the books told of many stunning encounters involving multiple witnesses, supported by radar returns and landing traces, medical effects (both injuries and healings) animal reactions, electromagnetic effects and more. I learned that the phenomena had been studied for decades and that there was an apparent cover-up by the US government which considered the subject Top Secret and of extremely high importance.

Finding out that UFOs were real was not good news. It hit me like a ton of bricks and caused me to reevaluate my entire worldview. Earth was being invaded by aliens and yet mainstream society seemed to be entirely ignorant of the fact.

I began to formally interview witnesses and decided to write an article for the local paper. I was surprised when the editor put the story on the front page of the Topanga "Messenger," making it the lead story. This brought in more reports. I began to subscribe to UFO magazines and journals and join any UFO groups I could find. I attended local meetings and conventions. Before long, I found myself actively investigating UFO incidents.

I began to write articles for various magazines and in 1996, wrote my first book. I began to appear on radio shows, which led to multiple television appearances.

In a few short years, UFOs had effectively taken over my life. Fast forward thirty years later, and I have now interviewed hundreds of witnesses and investigated UFO encounters of virtually every type. I have written twelve books about UFOs and six about the paranormal. I have also written more than 100 articles examining the various aspects of this very complex phenomenon.

One day I took all my articles out to review them and realized I was sitting on an enormous amount of UFO information. A good portion of my UFO research was available only in these articles, which were now very rare and difficult to find.

And so the idea for this book was born. This book is a collection of ten of my UFO articles, each representing the cutting edge of UFO research. Each article explores a different facet of the UFO phenomenon and is supported by firsthand cases.

My specialty--I think--has been the ability to review a large amount of data from a wide variety of sources and come up with unique insights and unusual patterns. With thirty years of UFO research under my belt, and more than 100 articles to choose from, the selection was based on several factors. I wanted to include some of my early work and some of my later articles. I also wanted to explore a wide variety of topics. My ultimate goal was to provide a comprehensive overview of the phenomenon, including everything from sightings and landings, to abductions, UFO crashes and stories of the government cover-up. I also had one rule: the articles would not contain information that's already available in one of my books.

All the articles in this book are original and have never been published in book form.

In "Conversations with Extraterrestrials," I explore cases in which people have held conversations with ETs, and learned information about their agenda on Earth.

"Phone Call from an Alien" explores a rare type of contact during which people receive phone calls or even radio messages from an extraterrestrial or UFO.

What happens when a person shoots a gun at a UFO? "UFO--Don't Shoot!" presents more than a dozen cases in which people have had a shoot-out with a UFO or alien.

It is well-known among UFO researchers that ETs are conducting an extensive study of our planet. "Alien Zoos" presents cases in which people have seen animals both earthly and extraterrestrial aboard UFOs.

"UFOs over Graveyards" is a spooky and sometimes bone-chilling look into cases in which UFOs have shown an undue interest in cemeteries.

While many people claim to have seen aliens aboard UFOs, much rarer are cases in which ETs have been seen mingling among the human population. "Aliens Among Us" presents more than a dozen cases in which ETs have been seen in some very unexpected places including subways, casinos, hotels, restaurants, bookstores and more.

"The Alien-Clown Connection" is a creepy expose of cases involving ETs who use the image of a clown (or something else) as a screen-memory in an apparent attempt to hide their identity.

Is it dangerous to investigate UFOs? "The Intimidation and Murder of UFO Witnesses" shows that having conclusive evidence or solid proof of UFOs can sometimes be a very dangerous thing.

The United States Government has been accused of withholding UFO hardware. "Exposed-- Project Redlight" presents a compelling case that the US Military has not only captured UFOs, but are actually flying them around.

In the final article, "Mining Data on UFOs," I explore one of the many alien agendas: cases in which UFOs target mines, apparently for the purpose of taking precious ores and metals from our planet.

While the articles in this collection have been previously published in various magazines and journals, they have never before been available in book form, and most of them have been edited to include new and current information. In addition to the articles, I have added a behind the scenes section in which I tell the story of how each article came to be written and in some cases the consequences that occurred after publication.

Finally, each article is illustrated by award winning UFO artist, Kesara.

This book presents the cutting edge of UFO research. Are you ready to learn the truth about UFOs?

Chapter One
Conversations with Extraterrestrials

One of the rarest types of UFO encounter is an onboard experience or a face-to-face encounter with an actual extraterrestrial. In my twenty years of UFO investigations, I have uncovered only a handful of these types of very close encounters. Surprisingly, in the vast majority of these encounters, there is little or no conversation between the humans and the aliens.

In the cases where there is conversation, it is often one-sided and limited to the extraterrestrials giving platitudes to the frightened witnesses. It's the same phrase over and over again. I've heard it a thousand times. It's almost like a broken record. The first word out of the aliens' mouths (or *minds*) is invariably, "DO NOT BE AFRAID. WE WON'T HURT YOU."

While the aliens are usually very tight-lipped, occasionally they will engage people in brief conversations or relay brief messages.

CASE ONE: "You Won't Remember This."

My first case involving conversations between humans and ETs occurred to the Robinson family of Reseda, California. In 1989, the family experienced a series of sightings and abductions by gray-type aliens, culminating in what UFO investigators call "a baby presentation." The main witness, Kelly Robinson, experienced four consecutive visitations over a period of a few

11

months. During each encounter, she was able to converse with the aliens.

On the first encounter, Kelly awoke to find four gray-type ETs standing around her bed. One spoke telepathically, telling her. "Do not be afraid. Come with us. You won't remember this."

Kelly, however, was a very feisty, independent twenty-year-old, and like twenty percent of abductees, she did remember. She recalled being taken into a small round room and placed on a table. They told her, "We're going to take your memory away. You'll not remember this...Don't be afraid. We're not going to hurt you. You can't remember this."

Kelly screamed at them, "Yes, I will!"

This argument went back and forth, with the aliens telling her she couldn't and wouldn't remember, and Kelly screaming back that she would.

They then cut her arm. She woke up the next morning and immediately looked at her arm. A neat two-inch scar was exactly where she remembered the aliens cutting her.

Two weeks later, the aliens returned, telling her, "We're going to take your memory."

Kelly screamed at them, "No, you're not. I'm going to tell."

They told her, "No, you're not...Your parents wouldn't understand. You better not tell them, you know."

Kelly screamed out that she would tell her father.

They said, "No, no, no! You can't."

A few weeks later, they came again. As usual, they attempted to erase her memory of the incident. They told her, "You're going to forget everything."

However, as usual, Kelly had some recall of the events. Says Kelly, "I don't know specifically what they asked me. They were asking me things about what we do, but you know, I can't specifically say. They [said,] 'this will happen and that will happen.' I think it's about my job or something."

Says Kelly, "It's hard for me to remember. They say, "You're going to forget everything.'...It's totally stressed on, "We're not going to let you remember this. We're going to take your memory of this away."

On her final encounter, the aliens appeared and said, "We need to talk to you. Come with us."

Kelly resisted and threatened to tell her father. They said, "No, you can't tell your dad."

Says Kelly, "I think they're religious. They're not really out to hurt us. They're out to learn. But they're afraid for us to remember because they're afraid we would tell people about them."

CASE TWO: "They Have Everything But Love."

Kelly Robinson's mother, Diane had an experience which she calls a "dream," but is clearly connected to the UFO encounters of her family. Diane recalls being taken into a room where she was shown babies that were genetically altered. First revealed by researcher Budd Hopkins, these rare cases involve abductees who are told to hold and nurture babies that appear to be half-alien and half-human. In most cases, there is little information

13

exchanged. Diane, however, was given a brief explanation.

She recalled being taken to a room where she saw a large contraption shaped like a Christmas tree, but instead of branches there were incubators filled with babies.

Diane was told to pick a baby and hold it. She refused because the babies appeared to be deformed. Says Diane, "Every one of them had something wrong with them. And she said it was sad, because it wasn't planned that way, that they had all these things wrong with them...She said they had everything but love. She said, 'That's why I'd like you to take one and love it...They have problems. They are different. But they still need love."

Diane was unable to overcome her revulsion and refused to hold the babies. Following this experience, all the UFO encounters of the Robinson family ended.

CASE THREE: "There's Going to be a Rebellion."

During my research into the UFO wave over Topanga Canyon, California (see *UFOs over Topanga Canyon*, Llewellyn, 1999), I uncovered several cases involving face-to-face extraterrestrial encounters. Again, in most cases, the aliens either didn't speak or said only, "Do not be afraid, we won't hurt you." However, in a few cases, messages were given. One case is that of the Martin family. It was Sarah Martin, the mother, who actually spoke with the extraterrestrials.

Sarah Martin's encounters occurred during the peak of the UFO wave and involved several close-up sightings and at least one onboard encounter. Sarah recalls being inside a small circular room surrounded by small robed figures. Says Sarah, "To be honest with you, I can't remember their faces. I just remember talking to them, and they were talking to me. And this is what they said: 'Why are you so involved in this [Ross Perot] campaign? Why are you wasting your time? It's going to fall apart, one by one, and whoever wins, it doesn't matter because the whole system is going to come down around everybody. There's going to be a rebellion. And you're not a part of this, so don't get involved.'"

At the time, Sarah was heavily involved in the Ross Perot presidential campaign. After the experience, she dropped all her political activities. Says Sarah, "This was so incredible. In my mind, I keep going over again what they said: 'You're not a part of this, so don't be a part of it. Get away from all of it.'...The other thing too is something about an earthquake, a big earthquake. Something like that...but the thing that stuck out the most was, 'Why are you so involved? Why are you letting this consume your time? It's not worth it, and it's all going to fall apart.'"

A few years later, the devastating Northridge earthquake struck, destroying several homes in Topanga Canyon.

CASE FOUR: "We Need Babies."

Interestingly, another Topanga witness received prophetic warnings of the Northridge earthquake the night before it occurred, thereby saving her from serious injury or even death.

Marcellina had had encounters all her life, but it wasn't until she moved into Topanga Canyon that she began to experience face-to-face visitations. Following the earthquake, she had an encounter with a gray-type extraterrestrial in her home.

During the encounter, the ET spoke to her telepathically. Says Marcellina, "It was telling me they were trying to invent ways of intercourse. They needed babies. It was just telling me a bunch of things telepathically. There would be more earthquakes. And then you know, we had all those earthquakes all over the world...I had changed my living room after the earthquake with a whole bunch of pictures I had painted of planets. And they told me that's not exactly the way it looked there...[they said] I would be able to heal myself and I would be able to heal them. If they wanted me to heal them, I would be able to heal them."

Following this experience, Marcellina experienced the missing-fetus syndrome. Well-known among UFO investigators, this syndrome involves women who become pregnant following a UFO encounter and then mysteriously lose the fetus. Marcellina also experienced subsequent paranormal healing events.

CASE FIVE: "Our Emotions Are Different Than Yours."

Pat Brown is a physical therapist from Panorama city, California. She had never thought of UFOs until 1992, when a vacation to Arizona triggered a series of encounters with gray-type extraterrestrials. For a period of several months, Pat

16

reported terrifying nightly visits by ETs in her condo. Then, one evening, she was taken onboard.

To her surprise, she found the experience enjoyable. She was given a tour of the craft and taken to meet "the master." It was then that she was given several messages of a spiritual nature. Says Pat, "I don't know all that they said to me, but I remember them telling me there was something I had to do with my aura."

She was surprised to find that the appearance of the alien had changed to a human male with blond hair. She asked, "Why do you look like that?"

The ET replied, "Because this is the way you want me to look."

Pat was taken out of her body and was shown what her astral body looked like. The ET told her, "That is your soul. That is the part of you that goes through all the lifetimes."

Pat was given further spiritual lessons on vibrations and healing and was then returned to her bedroom.

She soon had further experiences, and suffered several medical effects as a result of her encounters. Her case is also supported by additional witnesses. Her obsession with the subject grew and Pat began a search for information and was led to a channeler, someone claiming to speak for the ETs.

Pat asked the channeler if people who are abducted make an agreement on some level. The channeler, speaking for the ETs, said that yes, abductees do, in fact, agree to be abducted.

Pat said, "Can you make them stop?"

The ETs replied, "No, you cannot make them stop, but if you become consciously aware, you will be handled in a different way...You need to understand why you have created this. We perceive we are supporting you in your drama. Why did you create this?"

Another audience member asked, "You come here and you get specimens. What do we get from you?"

"You get a jumpstart in your growth. That's what we give you."

Another member asked about emotions and the ETs replied, "Our emotions are different than yours, but we do have emotions because we accept it as important to us."

The conversation continued until Pat became angry and shouted at them that they shouldn't take her against her will.

The ETs replied, "The experiences you are receiving from this far outweigh the other things you are experiencing, and there's not one person in this room that would not trade places with you."

Pat continues to have experiences, both positive and negative. She is also continuing her quest to understand the reasons for her encounters.

CASE SIX: "We Are From a Place You Don't Know About Yet."

In 1995, a middle-age couple, William and Rose Shelhart, were driving outside Sedona, Arizona late at night when they spotted a bright light in the sky following them. It soon became apparent that the light was playing a game of cat and mouse with them as it chased them down the road and eventually landed in a field next to them. That was the last thing they consciously remembered.

Their next memory was arriving at a hotel in Sedona, several hours too late. Realizing they had missing time, they later sought out a hypnotist and recalled an incredible onboard UFO experience. They recalled being taken onboard the craft and examined by nearly human-looking uniformed extraterrestrials. While William's recall was negligible, Rose was able to recall most of what happened, including an actual conversation that she had with the ETs.

According to Rose, they were "invited" onboard and treated with kindness and respect. Says Rose, "They [the extraterrestrials] were just saying that we are helping you. They told me [William] was in another room getting different messages."

Rose asked where they come from. The aliens gave a typically enigmatic and evasive answer, replying, "We are from a place you don't know about yet."

When asked about their purpose for coming here, their response was decidedly positive. Says Rose, "They said they are helping certain people here because they will help humanity. And something about like, the more we help, the more they help us. But they can't interfere and just take over and fix everything."

Rose was unable to obtain any further useful information. She and her husband continue to have sightings and encounters, and William reports that he was healed of carpel-tunnel syndrome as a result of his interaction with the ETs.

CASE SEVEN: "Don't Worry, We Won't Hurt You."

Jack Stevens (pseudonym), of Everett, Washington, was only twelve years old when he was abducted out of a car and into a large craft. Most of the event was shrouded in amnesia until 1997, when he spontaneously recalled what happened twenty-five years earlier. His memory revealed a harrowing six-hour-long abduction event.

Jack recalled being levitated inside a beam of light and placed on a table surrounded by short figures. As he was being taken onboard, the ETs told him, "Don't worry, we're not going to hurt you."

As they examined him, Jack reports that the aliens conversed among themselves. "I remember two of them going back and forth, and it was like a 'good cop, bad cop' thing. One of them, for all he cared, just throw me off. That's what the impression was, just, 'get him off here.' And the other one was saying, 'No, we are not going to do that.'

"I remember them telling me to open my mouth."

Jack became nervous about his mother and brother who were still back in the car. The beings responded, "Don't worry about it, we don't want them...Don't want them, don't need them...We don't care about them."

At one point, one of the beings attempted to relate a complex message. Says Jack, "He was telling me all kinds of stuff, but it wasn't sinking in. I didn't understand what he was telling me. There were math formula things and something about a lot of triangles and circles. There was a lot of geometry thrown at me. And I'm just sitting there thinking, this is pretty cool, but I kind of want to go home."

After several more procedures, the ordeal finally ended. As Jack was being placed back into his car, a final exchange ensued. Jack said, "You didn't do anything to my mom and brother, right?"

The beings responded, "Right, don't worry."

Jack's case involves considerable physical evidence and numerous other witnesses. The case is still ongoing.

CASE EIGHT: "We've been Here a Long, Long, Time."

A very unusual case of extraterrestrial contact occurred to a waitress named Maryann X, of Carpinteria, California. One evening in 1992, following a series of UFO sightings, Maryann was in her home watching TV when she became aware of a presence. Although she couldn't see anything, in her mind's eye she sensed a strange being. The figure was thin, bald, with a large head, gray skin and dark almond-shaped eyes, in other words, the typical gray-type alien.

At that point, Maryann began to experience the phenomenon of automatic writing. Messages which she believed were from the alien began to be transmitted through her.

Says Maryann, "He's very interested in our interest in him and his race. [He says] that they've been here for a long, long time, longer than we have from what I understand…They're vastly interested in us. They're almost more fascinated in us than we are in them. They're fascinated by us. We don't think the same way they do. He said, 'We live in oceans.' They live in the ocean, underwater. Their ships are underwater. They're very benign. They have no nuclear warheads [or] this kind of stuff."

Like many contactees, Maryann was given information about upcoming natural disasters. "He was telling me something about earthquakes. He didn't predict anything else. He just said we're in for some big type of natural disaster. I get the impression, thinking back to what he talks to me about, is that they're almost here to warn us. Not of an impending doom type of thing, like the world's going to blow up, but they're not here to hurt. They're here to observe."

The alien told Maryann that their race is much more numerous than all of humanity. "Lot and lots and lots. This is not just five or ten or twenty ships roaming around. We're talking--from what I get from him--millions and millions of these people. And they've existed before we recorded time and history."

The alien told her that they were conducting a program to contact small groups of people across the planet. "That's the understanding I have. They have jobs like everybody has jobs down here. His job is to find people who are receptive enough that he can talk to. And he was really worried about whether or not I was really scared...I get the impression that I am not the only one he talks to. In fact, I think that it's like a job for them. That's kind of the impression I got, is they kind of probe different people. It's like his job is to find people who are receptive."

Marianne has made contact with the alien on several occasions, and has been given much more information.

CASE NINE: "It Is Very Important We Do This."

Melinda Leslie of Los Angeles, California is an office manager and secretary who has been having ET contact her entire life. Even more amazing is that Melinda has been able to recall many of her experiences consciously, without the aid of hypnosis. She is what UFO researchers call a *conscious abductee.*

While she has had virtually the entire range of UFO experiences, one of her most dramatic occurred in July 1991 while driving with two friends through the Los Angeles forest. All three experienced a two-hour-long abduction into a metallic craft piloted by gray-type ETs.

Once on board, they were undressed, examined, separated and given separate messages. Melinda Leslie was able to recall the entire event consciously. As she was laid out and examined, she hammered the aliens with questions, none of which they answered.

She saw her friend sitting in a chair with a bizarre-looking headset on him and she screamed out, "What are you doing to him?"

One of the aliens replied, "It's all right, we're giving him information. It's all right. We're educating him."

"Don't hurt him," Melinda said.

23

"We're not hurting him. He's all right. It's all right."

Melinda continued to let out a stream of questions, however, she was rarely answered, and then, only in an evasive manner. Says Melinda, "They don't give you straight answers. They say, 'It's okay. We need to do this. You understand.'"

At one point, the three friends were separated and placed into different rooms. Melinda found herself in a room with a dozen grays. One stepped up to her and said, "Now, we're going to do something. Don't be afraid, but this is very important that we do this. We're going to put this over your head."

What followed was a bizarre procedure. Melinda was immobilized by a device placed over her head. The aliens stood in a circle around Melinda and pushed her back and forth like a punching clown. Melinda felt she was going to fall, but each time she was caught and pushed again. Finally, she relaxed. At that point, they stopped and removed the device. One of the aliens said, "You needed to learn that...You needed to learn to trust us."

Meanwhile, Melinda's friend, James was receiving a different message. Says Melinda, "James said when I was out of the room, they came over to him, and they showed him a device, a bunch of stuff. They told him how to make a UFO detector, and they gave him the information. He said, they said because they wanted him to document and videotape them. When sightings happen, they told him he has a mission to document this stuff."

According to James, "They showed me how to do this. And they explained the whole thing technically to me, and I was given the information how to build those. They were done and they made sure I understood. And I said, 'Yes, I understand.'"

Melinda's other friend was unable to recall much detail other than being taken onboard and examined. Melinda continues to have experiences and has lectured extensively about her encounters.

Conclusions

There are many other cases where aliens have conversed with human beings. However, the patterns are usually the same. For the most part, aliens are not only extremely taciturn; when they do speak they are often evasive. When abductee Travis Walton was taken onboard a UFO, he asked numerous questions of the aliens, none of which were answered. When abductee Betty Hill asked her abductors where they came from, they told her, "You wouldn't understand."

But as the above cases show, the aliens do sometimes reveal information about themselves, their feelings, their intentions, their desires, fears and beliefs. By piecing together these accounts, we are beginning to get a clearer picture of who the aliens are and what they are doing on this planet.

The main message revealed by the aliens' conversations is that they have a strong interest in humanity. Whether they are removing genetic material, imparting spiritual knowledge, predicting natural disaster or studying our emotions, the aliens are obviously fascinated by humanity. The conclusion is clear. For whatever reason, they are deeply interested in us. And if the patterns reveal anything, the aliens will remain here for a long, long time.

BEHIND THE SCENES: I broke one of my rules by including this article, as these cases are taken from my books. However, since there were so many accounts taken from several different books, I decided it would be okay. Also, this article turned out to be one of my more popular articles and reveals--I think--quite a bit about what it's like to be in contact with extraterrestrials. I wrote it because so many people ask me the same question: "Do the ETs ever say anything?" And as we have seen, they do converse with witnesses, but only rarely. The article appeared in Fate Magazine, June 2003, and was reprinted by request in the MUFON UFO Journal in their July 2003 issue.

After publication, researcher Billy Booth wrote, "I recently ran across one of the most well-written, informative, and well balanced articles I have seen in quite some time. I must give credit where it is due. A big thanks to Preston Dennett (California) field investigator for the Mutual UFO Network (MUFON). His "Conversations with Extra-terrestrials" is a must read for everyone interested in UFOs and Alien Contact. Dennett tells us that during his 20 years of research into UFOs, he has encountered only a few cases of direct alien contact. These are all very intriguing. The gist of his article is the actual conversation between humans and alien beings: mostly these are one-sided by the aliens.

Dennett brings up a very good point, and it is one that I have thought about before, but never elaborated on. In the vast majority of alien contact cases, there is little or no language exchanged, and often times simply transference of thought from the alien to the captive human…Dennett gives us a very good description of eight different cases that he has investigated which involve alien-human conversation. These are so interesting, you will want to read the entire article, which is quite lengthy, yet keeps your interest up the whole journey through. Don't miss this excellent piece of writing. You will gain some insight into the psyche of the alien intelligence, and how they tend to relate to us humans."

Chapter Two
Phone Call from an Alien

UFO contact comes in many different forms. Some people have sightings of craft. Others have onboard experiences. Some experience bedroom visitations with ETs. Others have only telepathic contact or even claim to channel ETs. But there is another form of contact that is so rare, there have been only a few reported cases. These unique cases involve UFO contact through a simple instrument found in most homes--the telephone. As bizarre as this sounds, enough accounts have turned up to merit a serious investigation.

Jack Sarfatti is today a prominent quantum physicist. Unknown to many, however, is that he may owe some of his success to a very unusual experience--a phone call from a flying saucer! The whole ordeal began more than fifty years ago.

Says Sarfatti, "In 1952 and 1953, when I was about twelve or thirteen years old, I received a phone call...in which a mechanical sounding voice at the other end said it was a computer on board a flying saucer. They wanted to teach me something and would I be willing? This was my free choice. Would I be willing to be taught--to communicate with them? I remember a shiver going up my spine, because I said, 'Hey, man, this is real.' Of course, I was kid...but I said, 'yes.'"

Sarfatti was impressed. He ran and got his friends, and they gathered together in his bedroom, awaiting the upcoming promised contact.

Unfortunately, nothing occurred and Sarfatti assumed at first that it was just a clever practical joke.

At this point, his memory of the event strangely ends. But according to Sarfatti's mother, the first phone call was followed by a series of similar phone calls--each giving Sarfatti information that would leave him forever changed. Says Sarfatti, "My mother remembers this experience very well. It turns out that I had forgotten most of it. This was really something that occurred over several weeks. Apparently what happened, which is completely blanked from my memory but not from hers, was that I continually received phone calls, many phone calls from the same source. My mother says I was walking around really strange. She began to get worried about me. Finally, one day she picked up the phone, and she heard this computer. She remembers the voices...She said, 'Leave my boy alone!' The Jewish mother talking to the flying saucer or whatever they were. My mother has a strong personality. And that was the end of it. We never got another phone call after that."

While Sarfatti is unable to consciously recall the messages given to him, his pioneering career as a quantum physicist may hold some of the answers. He championed Bell's theorem which is based on the Einstein-Rosen-Podolsky quantum physics experiments regarding the possibility that subatomic particles behave in a way that indicates some sort of "telepathic communication with each other." Einstein felt that such a possibility was "absurd." However, current experiments have proven, as

Sarfatti claimed, that subatomic particles are in fact connected with each other "non-locally." Sarfatti is today a leading authority on the physics of consciousness.

A remarkably similar case comes from the files of leading abduction investigator, Budd Hopkins. Debbie Jordan (aka: Kathie Davis of *Intruders*) has had a lifetime of UFO encounters in her rural Indiana home, including sightings, landings, abductions and more. And then, of course, there were the mysterious phone calls.

Starting in 1980, when she was pregnant with her second son, she began to receive a series of strange phone calls. The first one came on a Wednesday afternoon. Jordan answered the phone, but all she could hear was a roar "like a factory in full swing" and "a voice moaning and muttering but using no syllables she could understand."

She assumed somebody was playing a practical joke, and asked what was happening. When several solicitations received no response, she hung up the receiver and thought nothing further of it.

However, the next Wednesday, again at 3:00 o'clock in the afternoon, she received another identical phone call. Again there was a strange moaning voice with other odd noises. Again, she listened for a few moments and hung up. Following that, the phone-calls came regularly every Wednesday at about the same time. While she usually hung up, sometimes Debbie sat and listened with fascination to the "weird sounds."

On one occasion, Jordan's mother answered the phone and also heard "guttural sounds, the moaning, and the background roaring and clicking noises." On another occasion, Jordan's friend answered the phone and heard a strange voice. All the witnesses describe the voice as being sometimes angry, sometimes sad and sometimes neutral, talking in an unintelligible monologue. They couldn't tell if the voice was a man or a woman.

Finally, Jordan decided to have her phone number changed to an unpublished listing. She received her new unlisted number on a Monday. The next day, Tuesday, the mysterious phone caller rang. On this occasion, the voice sounded angry. It was the only time the mysterious calls ever came on any day other than Wednesday.

The calls continued for nine months, the entire duration of Jordan's pregnancy, then suddenly stopped. The ordeal was finally over. Or so she thought. Her son was thankfully born healthy and whole. However, by age three he had developed a strange speech problem. Instead of talking he would moan "much like the mysterious caller" who had plagued them for nine months. A battery of tests revealed no abnormality. Thankfully, he has grown out of the problem. But at the time, Jordan connected it to the phone caller, which she feels is somehow related to her UFO experiences.

Betty Andreasson is one of today's best-known UFO abductees. A half-dozen books have been written about her extensive UFO experiences. Not surprisingly, she has also experienced a few alien phone calls. It was October 19, 1977, and Andreasson was talking on the phone with her new friend Bob Luca (also an abductee,) whom she would later marry. Suddenly, a third party cut into their conversation.

Says Andreasson, "It's some of the *beings* and they're angry. Very angry. They broke into Bob's and my telephone conversation. And I can make out what they're saying: 'It's finished! It is done.' And they're really angry...They're talking very plainly but it's in a strange language, almost like a mad hornet. And I told them to speak up louder so that Bob could hear more clearly. And I heard--click, click--and they did speak louder. And it went--click, click, down--and they kept on speaking...and I'm hearing tones, like, ah, musical tones of some kind on the telephone."

Andreasson describes the phone call in familiar terms. As she says, "It was a different language. There was a lot of L's and a lot of T's in it and a lot of rolling sounds. It was fast, like a record was put on fast speed, but even though it was fast, the words were very clear. It was somebody very excited and quick...I could hear sort of a noise like some kind of heavy machinery was being set up...clickings and noises like they were putting things in order...Then that stopped, and they started talking again--and they were angry, just like an insect. It was like you would picture a mad hornet or an ant gouging away at something. The words just kept on going and repeating over and over."

Bob Luca was unable to distinguish any words. After a few moments, Andreasson became upset, so both she and Luca hung up the phone and called their respective investigators to report the strange incident.

Later that evening Andreasson was visited by ETs in her bedroom, who warned her of an upcoming tragedy in her family. Two days later, two of her children were killed in an automobile accident.

This was not the only occasion that the ETs used the phone to communicate with Andreasson. In 1973, in the middle of the night, she experienced a visitation in her Massachusetts home. She was still reeling from the encounter when the phone rang. A strange "high-pitched female voice" was on the line, asking for her husband. Whoever it was then immediately hung up. The phone call apparently worked as some kind of hypnotic device, for as a result, Andreasson completely forget the encounter that had just occurred and instead, returned to bed.

One of the most famous and controversial UFO cases of all times is that of Swiss farmer, Eduard Billy Meier. While investigating the case, Brit and Lee Elders and Wendelle Stevens experienced their own phone-related ET encounter.

It was in the early 1980s, and at the time, interest in the case was high. Because Stevens and the Elders were the lead investigators at the time, they found themselves the center of a lot of attention from a number of different intelligence services across the world. On one such occasion, the three researchers had been "politely invited" to a suite in the Grosvenor Hotel in London, to discuss the case with a "senior intelligence officer in one of the American services."

They showed up at the appointment, and met with a gentleman to discuss the case. They noticed that the office was very nicely furnished, and had two official-looking phones--one white and the other red. However, before any information could be exchanged, something strange happened.

Writes Stevens, "As soon as we were seated, and before any conversation was started the white phone rang *ten short rings!* I was jolted with surprise and I quickly looked at Lee and Brit, who were also looking surprised. Our interviewer picked up the phone and was trying to get an answer, but apparently there was nobody on the line. Recovering, I asked the gentleman if his phone ever rang like that before. He said it was a strange ring all right, as he was still trying to get an answer on the other end of the line, but now it clearly seemed to be dead. I suggested somebody playing tricks and he said he could find out, and dialed the operator and asked what happened to the call that came through."

The gentleman told the operator that he had been cut off. The operator, however, replied that no calls had been directed to his phone, and that if one had, the switchboard would have lit up. The gentleman hung up the phone.

Stevens describes what happened next: "He cleared his throat and turned to start the conversation again, when the red phone rang *ten short rings!* He grabbed the phone and quickly answered it as though he would catch the caller this time. Again no answer. This time there was no mistaking the ring. Our interviewer said, 'I can't believe this! I'll get to the bottom of it right now. This is a direct line right to telephone central. It bypasses the switchboard downstairs and goes through no other operators. It is a secure line and only especially cleared people can use it."

The gentleman called the operator again and verified that no calls had been sent to the line. According to Stevens, he was definitely perplexed, saying only, "This is very strange."

To Stevens, however, the message was clear. As he writes, "This situation was only one of more than a dozen such, of different kinds, which clearly demonstrated to us that the Pleiadians were aware of everything that we were doing, as well as everything anybody else was doing that may pertain to them in any way. They alone knew who all the players were."

Throughout the 1980s, the Robinson family of Reseda experienced a series of UFO sightings while camping in the San Bernardino Mountains. What started with sightings, however, escalated into a more extensive encounter. It was in December 1987 when their youngest daughter, Kelly (age 24) had a bedroom visitation by grey-type ETs, who abducted her into a UFO. This was followed by more encounters, which soon began to spread to other members of the family. The whole ordeal culminated in what researchers call a "baby presentation" in which the mother was apparently taken onboard a craft and made to hold and nurture apparent human-alien hybrids.

Like other abductees, the family experienced some poltergeist-like activity. And then, of course, there were the phone problems in Kelly's room.

Kelly reports that the phone in her room makes a loud dinging noise at three am, on an almost nightly basis. The noise sounded like somebody lifting and setting down the receiver. One time after it dinged, Kelly quickly answered the phone, and the line was dead.

The strangest incident occurred right before one of her close encounters. She woke up to hear the phone dinging. She then discovered that the phone was inside a paper bag, in her drawer. It hadn't been there when she went to bed. She then had her third bedroom visitation with ETs.

Kelly doesn't know what to make of the odd phone-effects. It's only one of many bizarre happenings that occurred over the two-year period of 1986 to 1987. She does admit that she wondered if the phone calls were from UFOs or even ghosts. But the thought scared her and she pushed it out of her mind. Today thankfully, the encounters have ceased.

If ETs can tap into phone lines with ease, then there should also be cases where they have used other instruments, such as radios and stereos to communicate. Certainly the technology to achieve this type of contact must be available to the alleged ETs. As it turns out, there are a few such cases.

One example comes from famed UFO abductee Whitley Strieber, author of *Communion*. In his book, he describes a wide variety of contact experiences, including one involving his stereo.

Writes Strieber, "One evening in April 1977, something so bizarre happened that I still cannot understand why we didn't make more of it. With both of us [Strieber and his wife, Anne] sitting together in our living room, somebody suddenly started speaking through the stereo, which had just finished playing a record. We were astonished, naturally, when the voice held a brief conversation with us. The voice was entirely clear, not like the sort of garbled message sometimes picked up from a passing taxi's radio or a ham operator. Never before had it happened, and it didn't happen again. I do not remember the conversation, except the last words: 'I know something else about you.' That was the end. I was left dangling."

The Striebers looked at each other in astonishment. Had they just received a stereo message from an ET? Even more puzzling, did they just have an interactive conversation? Whitley did his best to investigate. As he writes, "We did not completely ignore the incident. I called the Federal Trade Commission. A man explained to me what I already knew, that ham radios and taxis and police radios sometimes interrupt stereos. But a conversation, he asserted, was impossible. Our stereo had neither a microphone nor a cassette deck. It was a KLH, a good and relatively inexpensive model readily available in the mid-seventies. At the time, I'd had it for about four or five years."

A few weeks later, the Striebers moved. But within one year, they had more ET-phone related problems. Writes Strieber, "In June 1978 something terrible happened in the middle of the night. I have variously thought of it as a phone call followed by a menacing visit, and as a series of menacing phone calls. I do know that I called the police, and they came up and checked out the roof, finding nothing. I remember only looking out our bedroom window onto the roof garden and seeing somebody standing there. Just a prowler, perhaps, but it has always seemed to me that there was more to it than that." A few weeks later, the Striebers moved again.

In some cases, the ETs give friendly messages. In other cases, they give warnings. One case involving the latter comes from researcher Harold T. Wilkins, who writes that in January 1954, numerous people across the United States and the world received a strange message on their radio sets. Writes Wilkins, "In a car parked in a Middle Western town, a 'dead' radio receiver suddenly came to life and a voice said, 'I wish no one to be afraid, although I speak from outer space. But if you do not stop preparations for war, you will be destroyed.' On a radio hook-up last night, a newscaster says this message has been heard both in Los Angeles...something very similar happened over a radio transmission line at the London airport in January 1954. The mystery of that transmitting voice remains unsolved."

In 1960, sixteen-year-old Edwin X of Durban, South Africa was approached by a human-looking man who claimed to be an extraterrestrial. Edwin was skeptical, but the man promised to prove his assertions. He took Edwin to the coast and arranged a UFO contact. To Edwin's surprise, a UFO showed up just as his ET friend said it would. Says Edwin, "I saw to my amazement a bright light above the water coming towards us. It grew larger as it approached...it stopped and changed course...it stopped again and hovered...it was a beautiful spectacle. I was quite over-awed."

After convincing Edwin of his ET ancestry, his friend gave him a portable radio set and told Edwin that they would use it to contact him. While there were a few further face-to-face contacts, soon his ET friend would leave forever.

One month later, Edwin began receiving messages on his radio set. These messages continued for a period of no less than seventeen years, and cover a wide range of topics including astronomy, history, physics, time-travel, earth changes, the ETs themselves (they call themselves Koldasians, and are part of a "Confederation" of species) and more. Edwin not only recorded the messages, he formed a small research group around him, including Karl van Vlierden, who later published a book detailing the case.

How are these messages transmitted? Says Edwin, "To make a transmission, the spacecraft takes up a position directly above our house. They are approximately 520 km above the ground, but are not visible to the naked eye. On some occasions they come lower especially to show themselves to us, but for radio transmissions they remain at about that height. To communicate they send down a narrow beam, like a beam of light, but of course it is invisible. I think that's how they energize the receiver, by beaming the power the transistors need, and this beam carries the message. The receiver does not need to be tuned to any particular frequency. I have added a switch to cut off the front end (RF stage) of the set. This is the reason no other receiver can pick up these transmissions, unless they know one's location and the antenna is connected to the final stage."

Writes group member Karl van Vlierden, "Other methods of communication have been tried by the Confederation. For example, in about May 1979 Edwin's sister-in-law was recording pop music from the radio. On playback she discovered a cryptic message inserted in the recorded music. A voice clearly spoke these words: 'We come in peace...We can do these things on tape recorders. We come in peace and soon all shall be well. We are monitoring you...'"

Further proof of the validity of the case surfaced when Edwin was able to photograph the Koldasian craft on May 29, 1973. Numerous other members of his group, and his family and friends, have also seen the craft. The case was researched by Ruth Rees who writes, "This unique form of radio communication with the Confederation continued for seventeen years until one day in early 1979, three Security Branch members of the South African police visited Edwin's home and confiscated his radio. Many weeks later when Edwin contacted the police asking for the return of the unit, they denied ever having it and ever sending anyone around to confiscate it!"

Karl Van Vlierden's book, *UFO Contact From Planet Koldas: A Cosmic Dialogue* gives a comprehensive presentation of the case, including extensive verbatim messages from the ETs and photographs of the craft.

A particularly chilling case comes from an abductee based in New York. Kenneth has had contact his entire life, including several episodes of missing time.

Sometimes, before an abduction episode, the ETs would warn Kenneth telepathically of their impending arrival. If hearing voices in his head wasn't strange enough, on one occasion, the ETs decided to call him by cell-phone. In August 2006, Kenneth was driving home from work at about 3:00 am. He had his cell phone with him, just in case the car broke down. Suddenly, the phone started beeping a series of random tones. The ringer was set on a particular song, and had actually never made these kinds of tones before. Kenneth picked up the phone and answered it. The line was totally dead. He shut off the receiver, shut the phone, and put it back on the front seat.

Moments later, it started beeping weirdly again. Kenneth picked it up and looked at the digital screen to see who was calling. It read: NO NUMBER. He answered the call. Says Kenneth, "I heard funny clicking noises, not like a mechanical click, more like a person with their tongue at the roof of their mouth and then snapping it down--that kind of click. But it was very rapid. I thought, *Wow, this is nuts!* I began to get a little freaked. And I heard a voice say, 'The time has grown closer.' I got so scared, I didn't even realize I was going 90 miles an hour."

Kenneth hung up the phone and threw it on the seat. He raced back home at top speed, and tried to ignore the creepy feeling that he was being watched and hunted. He saw a small white sphere darting around, but decided to just ignore it. *We know where you are*, the voices sounded in his head.

42

Be prepared, we are coming soon. Soon you will know the reason. Shortly later, Kenneth experienced the most profound abduction event of his life.

Another case was researched by Canadian investigator Grant Cameron. The witness was Wilbert Smith who headed Project Magnet, the Canadian UFO research from 1950 to 1954. Smith says that he was in communication with an ET named AFFA. Some of the messages from AFFA were channeled by a medium, while others came from the phone. At the time, Smith was working on a gravity control experiment based on information from AFFA. At one point, AFFA called and told Smith, "Shield the experiment." Smith followed the advice and built a large brick-wall shield around the experiment, which later exploded and would have caused extensive damage.

While these cases are admittedly very rare, they actually fit neatly into the pattern of UFO contact. UFOs are known for their ability to produce a wide range of electromagnetic effects including stopping car engines, causing static on radios or interference on television screens, or even causing widespread power outages. Also, researchers have long been aware that ETs are, in fact, tapping in on our conversations.

Writes Major Donald Keyhoe, "There is evidence that the aliens not only hear our radio but also understand at least some messages. In numerous cases, when AF flight commanders or tower operators radioed pilots to close on UFOs or try to box them in, the alien machines have instantly reversed course or performed other evasive maneuvers. After the 1952 action at Washington Airport, veteran Traffic Controller Jim Ritchey told me of identical UFO reactions. When he radioed a Capital Airlines pilot to make a quick turn toward the nearest unknown object it shot straight up, accelerating from 130 to 500 miles an hour in four seconds. The same thing happened twice when Senior Controller Harry Barnes radioed pilots to attempt interceptions. Barnes later told me he was certain that the unknown visitors were listening to his instructions. A similar incident was reported by a Marine Corps squadron leader, Major Charles Scarborough, after an incident with sixteen flying discs over Texas. With all the US and foreign reports on record, the evidence appears conclusive."

Clearly if UFOs can do this with radios, they would also have the ability to affect telephone lines. UFOs have often been seen hovering directly over telephones wires. Perhaps they are not only siphoning off electricity, but are listening in, and sometimes making themselves known. Many abductees have reported a wide variety of phone problems. Usually these problems are attributed to government agencies tapping the phone lines. But the above cases suggest that it may be the ETs who are doing the tapping.

Longtime investigator John Keel is well aware of the bizarre connection between UFOs and weird phone calls, and has received a few himself. He describes several cases of UFO witnesses and investigators who have received calls involving "mechanical sounds" "high-pitched whining, beeping sounds" and other garbled or high-speed voices.

Writes Keel, "As for strange phone calls, I have investigated so many that I am now practically a telephone engineer."

In his book, *The Mothman Prophecies,* he quotes several accounts in which people have received phone calls in conjunction with UFO sightings. Writes Keel, "Voices counting off meaningless numbers also cut in on TV reception in UFO flap areas...another version of this phenomenon are the Morse code-like beeps that blast out of car radios, telephones, and TV sets when UFOs are active...Sometimes after watching an object, their telephones will suddenly ring, and there will be no one on the line...Obviously these things are manifestations of the electromagnetic spectrum. The voices, however, seem to come from a more mysterious superspectrum."

Keel points out that several UFO abductees have reported amnesia after hearing strange beeping tones, and he speculates that the strange beeping tones on the telephone may serve as a hypnotic suggestion from the ETs. This certainly seems to be true in Andreasson's case.

Longtime researcher Grant Cameron has also written about these bizarre cases. "Do aliens use the phone?" he asks. "It seems strange that with so much technology on their side they would revert to using a telephone, but there are actually a lot of stories of aliens not calling home, but calling people who are witnesses or who have chosen to investigate the UFO phenomena. Why would aliens use the phone? One possible answer is that we are not telepathic and they are forced to communicate using our standard of communication."

Whatever the explanation, these accounts show that the UFOs are using a wide variety of methods to make contact, and are influencing people in ways we have yet to understand.

BEHIND THE SCENES: "Phone Call from an Alien" was originally published in Fate Magazine in their April 2006 issue. I wrote the article after encountering a few of my own cases involving this strange aspect of the UFO phenomenon. I was honestly shocked by the information I was able to find and it definitely expanded my view of how strange and bizarre UFO contact is and the many different ways it can take place. And while the cases may seem unbelievable, the fact that there are so many makes them difficult to deny. And certainly UFO are known for affecting all kinds of electromagnetic machines including causing radios and televisions to become full of static, causing car engines to fail, or even causing widespread power outages.

After completing the article, I sent it off to Fate magazine and to my delight, it got the cover. Billy Booth of UFOs-About.com reviewed the piece and called it "a great article...a superb piece of writing and a wealth of information." Thanks, Billy!

Often UFO researchers will discover the same patterns, so I wasn't surprised when years later I discovered an article by longtime researcher, Grant Cameron focusing on the same types of cases. Cameron presented some of the same cases in my own article, and several new ones. And if trends continue as they have, soon there will be more people receiving a phone call from an alien.

48

Chapter Three
UFO: Don't Shoot!

When confronted with the unknown, it seems to be a basic law of human nature to shoot first and ask questions later. Rightly or wrongly, many of us perceive the unknown as a threat, and take appropriate precautions to protect ourselves--fight or flight. Given the prevalence of firearms in modern society, the expression of self-protection often involves a gun of some sort. And given further that UFOs represent the unknown--if anything does!--it should come as no surprise that there are several occasions when humans have taken up arms against these strange flying objects and/or their occupants.

What happens when the interaction between humans and UFOs escalates to violent conflict? What happens, for example, when a person actually fires a gun at a UFO or shoots at an alleged entity? For that matter, what happens when the UFO fires back? Let's examine the record of shoot-outs between humans and unidentified flying objects.

One of the first recorded cases of a UFO being fired upon occurred on February 25, 1942. It was only a few months after the Japanese bombing of Pearl Harbor when Los Angeles was invaded by several large UFOs hovering overhead. The entire city enforced a mandatory blackout while the military scrambled to confront what they thought were Japanese aircraft. The UFOs were caught in the beam of several search lights, and the military proceeded to fire upon the objects. Altogether about

1,430 rounds of ammunition were fired at the aerial objects with no visible effect whatsoever. On the ground, however, it was a different story: several buildings and homes were extensively damaged and at least six civilians died, resulting in a subsequent Congressional investigation.

A similar event reportedly occurred in the Soviet Union on July 24, 1957. Several UFOs were sighted over the Kouril Islands and Russian anti-aircraft batteries went into action. The repeated attacks failed to bring down any UFOs.

There are also cases where jet-fighters have fired upon UFOs. One example occurred when two F-6s were scrambled to intercept a UFO that had appeared on radar, clocked at a speed of 700 MPH. At top speed, one of the jets was able to approach within 500 yards of the object, which then began to outdistance the jets. At a distance of 1,000 yards, the pilot fired his guns at the UFO. Not surprisingly, the UFO was unaffected by the gunfire and vanished quickly in the distance.

Another jet fighter that had a shoot-out with a UFO occurred on September 19, 1976 over Tehran, Iran. On that day, a bright glowing object was seen by hundreds of people as it maneuvered over the city. The Iranian Air Force scrambled two F-4 phantom jets to chase the object. The pilot of the first jet lost instrumentation and communication when he approached the object.

The second pilot was General Parviz Jafari. He watched the object dart around more than 26 miles in less than a second. Suddenly a smaller object separated from the larger object.

The smaller object headed directly toward Jafari. He instinctively fired at it. Immediately all the instruments failed and his radio went dead. Says Jafari, "I was very frightened." Jafari wondered if he was going to have to eject when suddenly his instrument panel and radio began working again, and he was able to safely land.

There are many cases on record where normal hand-guns have been used against UFOs. On June 26, 1972 at Fort Beaufort, South Africa, police were reported to have fired upon a "glowing metallic object" from only eight yards away. Upon being shot at, the UFO made a humming sound and took off. Although the gunfire affected the UFO, it apparently did not harm it.

In 1953 a man in South Carolina was drawn out of his home because his animals were acting disturbed. He also heard a strange sound, upon which he saw an "egg-shaped object hovering over his barn." The object began to move away, at which point the man grabbed his gun and fired several shots. He heard the bullets strike the object, but again no obvious damage was observed.

In May 1964, the small virtually unknown town of Rio Vista (then a population of about 2000 persons) experienced a two-year-long wave of sightings, as reported by hundreds of local residents. Starting early in the month, witnesses began seeing a torpedo-shaped object about five feet wide and twelve feet long. It glowed bright red and moved silently at treetop level through the town.

It appeared so regularly throughout the month, that residents were able to predict its appearance. As a result, one witness was able to obtain color photographs of the object, which she eventually presented to the local sheriff's office. The object usually appeared above a particular water-tower about five miles outside of town, where it would hover less than fifty feet above the ground.

One of the first dramatic sightings occurred on May 13, 1964 in the small town of Rio Vista, California when an anonymous female resident reported that she saw two objects – both described as round and luminous. One of the objects came down and landed in a nearby field.

Many others in the town began to see the object which seemed to be attracted to the town's water-tower. Before long, two teen-agers saw the object. They took their .22 rifles and shot at the object. The witnesses are sure that the bullets found their mark as they both heard a metallic "twang" as the bullets hit, and the object flared up brightly in response.

Still, the craft continued to visit the water tower, and would do so regularly for the next two years. Later, in 1965, a remarkable encounter would involve nearly the whole town and would generate interest from Air Force officials.

Another case is that of Michael Campeadore. On May 13, 1967 near St. George, Utah, Campeadore was driving when he became aware of a strange humming sound. He pulled over and exited his car, looked up and saw a "huge object" about fifty feet in diameter hovering over him. Frightened by the object, he retrieved a .25 caliber pistol from his car and started shooting. He, too, heard the bullets strike their target, but again the UFO rapidly departed without any apparent harm.

It was late at night on July 19, 1967 when Jack Hill (age 60), nightwatchman for the Lumber Consolidated Company in Wilmington, encountered a UFO. He was patrolling the grounds when he observed a fifty-foot long metallic craft covered with lights hovering only a few hundred feet away. To his shock, the strange object zoomed straight towards him. Hill took immediate defensive action. His fight or flight instincts prevailed, and as he couldn't flee, he decided to shoot first and ask questions later. He speedily drew his service revolver and fired six shots at the object in quick succession. Says Hill, "Then the lights of the craft went out and it flew away." The craft apparently was unharmed. Hill, on the other hand, was impressed enough that he later told his story to reporters at the *Los Angeles Herald Examiner.*

Not all cases of UFO shoot-outs involved just objects. At other times people have been known to fire on UFO occupants.

On October 1973, Paul Brown, a car dealer in Athena, Georgia may have prevented an actual UFO abduction by shooting at the aliens. The ordeal began as Brown was driving late at night and his radio was suddenly filled with static. At the same time, a bright light lit up the interior of his car. Moments later a "strange craft" about fifteen feet in diameter landed ahead of him on the road. Brown skidded to a halt and watched as two creatures exited the UFO and began to walk towards him. Brown describes them: "They were about four feet tall. They looked like they were wearing silver uniforms, including their shoes. There was some elastic at their ankles and the suits were closed tight at the neck also. They had silver gloves, and their hair was solid white." Fearing a possible abduction, Brown grabbed his pistol from his car and aimed it at the aliens. The aliens quickly returned to their craft. As they entered, Brown opened fire on the UFO, which promptly took off.

On September 4, 1964, Donald Shrum and two companions were hunting in the wilderness outside Cisco Grove, California when Shrum became separated and lost. As evening approached, he realized that he would have to spend the night outside. Knowing there were bears in the area, he climbed a tree where he planned to stay. Shortly later, he saw a strange star-like object drop out of the sky. It approached him and he saw it was actually a craft with three strange panels on the side. Suddenly, a smaller craft was ejected from one of the panels. The smaller craft dropped down and landed about a half-mile away. It wasn't long afterwards that Shrum saw a strange figure approaching him.

The figure was five feet tall, helmeted with large goggles, and wore a white uniform. It came to the area where Shrum was and began to examine the Manzanita plants. Shortly later it was joined by another and later, four others.

At first they didn't seem to notice Shrum, but when they did, Shrum's shoot-out began. A strange robot-like figure approached and began to emit noxious gas which rendered Shrum momentarily unconscious. Shrum tried to keep them away by throwing down burning matches and bits of cloth. He threw his canteen at them.

The robot-like figures were not discouraged and continued to try and dislodge Shrum. Fearing he was about to be abducted, Shrub took out his bow and arrow and began shooting. It was a 60-pound recurve bow with a 28-inch pull. At close range, the velocity of the arrow is comparable to a bullet. Says Shrum, "I tried shooting the robot with my bow...I just pulled it back as far as I could, and hit him the first time."

There was a big flash of light and the robotic figure fell backwards about ten or twenty feet. At the same time, the uniformed humanoids retreated and scattered. Says Shrum, "I guess it scared them a little."

The robot returned and Shrum shot two more arrows at it. Each time, there was a bright flare of sparks as the arrow struck the metallic body of the robot, which again fell backward several feet.

Unfortunately, the arrows weren't able to keep the robotic creature away and it returned each time. Luckily for Shrum, however, their techniques didn't work. Eventually the creatures left, returned to their craft, which joined the larger mother ship, which took off upwards and disappeared.

Probably the most famous UFO shoot-out of all time occurred to the Sutton family of Hopkinsville, Kentucky. The ordeal began on the evening of August 22, 1955, when one member of the family sighted a glowing object landing in a field behind the house. Moments later the entire family saw a three-foot-tall humanoid creature with huge eyes, ears and clawed hands approaching the house. Suddenly several of the creatures appeared at once, and the alarmed family ran inside. One of the creatures appeared on the roof and grabbed at one of the family members. At that point, Frank Sutton, the father of the family, fired a shotgun through the screen door at one of the creatures. It was a direct hit, and the creature was knocked over by the blast; however, it instantly jumped back up and scampered away. The creature continued to terrorize the family, who finally piled into their car and drove to the police. The police and the family returned to the location of the incident, but there was no evidence of the creatures. The police left, and shortly later, the creatures came back. The family remained inside while the creatures roamed outside, finally leaving hours later. This incredible incident is very famous in the annals of Ufology, having been recounted in several books. As always seems to be the case, the aliens were not harmed in any way by the gunfire.

Yet another case which involved an alleged alien entity--in this case a Bigfoot-like alien--occurred in Fayette County, Pennsylvania. In October of 1973, the local police began receiving several calls concerning UFOs. Three witnesses said they saw a ball of light land in a nearby field. One of the witnesses, Stephen Meacham was armed with a 30-06 rifle, and the three of them went to investigate. Upon approaching the area, the three sighted "two hairy creatures" in the field. Meacham fired three rounds of ammunition at them that had no apparent effect. Meacham is positive his bullets

56

struck the creatures. They turned and looked at him, but didn't noticeably alter their pace.

The police were called and a single officer was sent to investigate. Meacham and the officer encountered the creatures face-to-face, with Meacham again doing the shooting. "I shot directly into the chest of the creature," he said. "It swayed backward, and then came right at the fence."

Again the bullet did not seem to harm its intended target. "I had to hit them," Meacham added, "but it didn't faze them. They kept the same gait. They never hurried."

On February 6, 1974, near Uniontown, Pennsylvania, a very similar incident occurred. It began when Mrs. A. heard what she thought were wild dogs. She ran and got her 16-gauge shotgun and went outside. She was immediately confronted by a "seven-foot tall, hair-covered, ape-like creature standing just six feet away." The creature raised both its hands, as if to attack, so Mrs. A. fired the gun into the creature's mid-section. Then the creature reportedly "just disappeared in a flash of light."

Mrs. A. ran back inside, and her son-in-law living next door called her on the phone. She told him the story, and he ran outside armed with a six-shot revolver. As he approached Mrs. A.'s house he saw "shadows of four or five hairy people" with "fire-red eyes that glowed." He fired two shots at them to no effect. Running inside he and his mother-in-law spotted a "bright red flashing light" in the woods a short distance away.

Still another case involving the shooting of Bigfoot occurred near Point Isabel, Pennsylvania in the fall of 1988. Three men sighted a Bigfoot-like creature outside a farmhouse and went looking for it. One of the men, Arnold Hubbard, was armed with a .22 rifle. At one point the creature was only fifty feet away from the men, and Hubbard fired a direct hit at the creature. The creature let out a "hideous scream" and Hubbard fired two more shots. Suddenly it became enveloped in a "white mist" and when the mist dissipated, the creature was gone. One of the witnesses to the incident, Larry Abbott, said, "The three of us searched the spot where the creature was shot that night. We found no trace of it, no blood, nothing. The next day we checked the whole farm, nothing."

There are a few cases where people have attempted to shoot at UFO occupants only to be defeated by mysterious means. One such case happened on July 15, 1979 to a couple in San Antonio, Texas. The couple sighted three large glowing balls of light outside their home. As they watched, five creatures described as "thin, with grayish skin, large hands and large, oval-shaped, slanted eyes" descended from the balls of light. The man ran and got his shotgun, at which point both the man and the woman were overcome with sleepiness.

Later under hypnosis a frightening abduction was remembered; at the time, however, the couple experienced only a period of missing time. Their next memory is waking up in the morning to find the shotgun completely dismantled, lying on the kitchen table.

Evidently the aliens had taken the gun and pulled it apart for examination. As usual, the weapon had no effect, certainly not to the extent of preventing an apparent abduction from taking place.

The military has also tried to shoot at UFOs, only to be mysteriously thwarted. The following incident was reported to have occurred in 1954, of the coast of Binn, Korea. It was during the Korean war, and the US Air Defense Artillery had several Hawk missiles set up in the event of an attack by the North Koreans.

At 10:00 AM, a blip was spotted on radar, moving towards the base. The officers on the base soon sighted the object which was described as a "glowing metallic disk, estimated to be 100 yards in diameter, ten yards high, with red and green pulsating lights moving around the rim counterclockwise."

The craft had approached within 700 yards of the base when the captain of D Battery gave orders to launch a Hawk missile. Before it could reach its target, the UFO reported replied with "a beam of white light," disabling the Hawk. The UFO then departed, making a sound "like a swarm of bees."

Some people who have taken pot-shots at UFOs soon find that they regret it. Assuming UFOs represent a superior technology, terrestrial weapons, especially handguns and rifles, would appear to be an extremely primitive form of defense at best. Nevertheless, on occasion UFO occupants apparently feel threatened enough by gunfire to respond in kind. What happens when they do?

Consider first an incident that took place on November 14, 1954 in Isola, Italy. A local farmer watched as a "cigar-shaped craft" landed nearby, disgorging three small beings dressed in "diving suits" who promptly surrounded his rabbit cages. Fearing for his animals, the farmer retrieved his gun and aimed it at the invading dwarfs. At that point, the gun became "so heavy in [his] hands that he had to drop it." Now, unable to move or cry out, he could only watch helplessly while the diminutive beings took his rabbits and returned to their craft. As soon as it lifted off, he could move again. He quickly squeezed off a round of bullets, but the object was now too distant to have any discernible effects.

Presumably the UFO occupants became aware of the farmer's intentions and rendered them ineffective by some sort of physical paralysis. According to some reports, other individuals have not been so fortunate.

In another case, two hunters shot at a UFO, only to have it shoot down a beam of light. As investigated by researcher Brian Vike, on a January evening in 1976, two men were driving along a remote dirt road on their way to go hunting coyotes in the desert outside of Clovis, New Mexico. Ahead of them they saw a bright blue-green light at a low altitude. There had been recent UFOs in the area, and it looked they were seeing one for themselves. They continued to drive and were able to drive right underneath the object, which appeared to be less than a thousand feet high. At this point, they exited the truck to take a closer look.

Writes Vike, "Since the men both had rifles with them, the witness I talked with grabbed his 30-06 rifle and took a shot at the object and believes he put a round into it. As soon as the fellow fired and the impact of the shell struck the craft it immediately started to move straight north."

The two men now found themselves hunting UFOs instead of coyotes. They hopped into their truck and followed the object as it moved towards Clovis. Although they moved at top speed, the object easily outdistanced them until it was two miles ahead.

They continued to follow it until they saw a police car up ahead with its emergency lights flashing, apparently also chasing the object. As they watched, the object shot down a bright beam of light "completely flooding the squad car with light."

At this point the object darted upwards and was gone. Writes Vike, "He [one of the hunters] told me he sat quietly by because he figured it might have been a military aircraft and he just put a bullet into the thing, not wanting to get into any trouble over shooting it. Also he mentioned after he saw the object doing all these strange maneuvers, he was glad he placed a bullet into it."

On October 18, 1973, truck driver Eugenio Douglas was nearing Monte Maix, Argentina when he was stunned and temporarily blinded by a bright beam of light coming from above. As Douglas pulled off the road, a "glowing disk" landed on the highway and "four things like shiny metal robots" moved towards him. Douglas realized that they were probably attempting to abduct him. Grabbing his loaded revolver, he fired point-blank at the advancing entities. "The bullets seemed to have no effect on them," Douglas said, so "I took off running across the countryside."

Douglas fled towards the nearest civilization. As he did, the disk followed him, swooping low. "Each time that disk made a pass over my head," he said, "I felt a blast of roasting heat." By the time Douglas made it to safety, huge blisters had formed on his back. While the case is famous for the injuries suffered by the witness, fortunately his injuries were not fatal. Others have not been as lucky.

On August 13, 1967, in the state of Goias, Brazil, Inacio de Souza and his wife Maria returned to their home to see a giant object, thirty-five meters in diameter landed on their property. The UFO was described as a "strange object shaped like a basin, only upside down." The couple then sighted three "strangers" that Inacio at first thought were nude. Maria, however, thought they were wearing tight-fitting yellow suits. The figures--who were all bald--saw that they were being observed and ran straight for the frightened couple. Inacio told his wife to run inside, then took his gun and shot the nearest creature. At that moment, he was struck in the chest by a beam of green light and fell to the ground. His wife returned and grabbed the rifle. All three intruders then quickly returned to their craft which "took off vertically with the noise of a swarm of bees."

For two days, Inacio experienced nausea and full-body numbness. He felt burning hot and weak. His symptoms progressed and became worse and finally, he went to a doctor who said that he must have eaten a "noxious plant." Inacio told his doctor about the UFO encounter, and the doctor immediately ordered more tests, including a blood test. The blood tests supposedly revealed a condition very similar to leukemia. Inacio was told that he had about two months to live.

As the doctor predicted, Inacio DeSouza rapidly lost weight and became sicker. In less than two months he was dead.

What do the above cases tell us about UFOs and their presumed occupants when fired upon? More cases could be listed, but the patterns are clear. In terms of "fight or flight," UFOs, it seems, prefer to flee rather than engage in an exchange of gunfire. On rare occasions, however, UOs have returned tit-for-tat, and have taken active measures to ensure that they weren't harmed--actions which have occasionally resulted in harm to humans. On a few occasions, they appear to have responded with violent reprisals aimed at the offending individual.

Whatever the ultimate nature of UFOs, one lesson seems perfectly clear: there is not a single case in which gunfire resulted in permanent damage of a UFO or its reported occupants. Nor are there any cases in which the UFO has ever fired first.

In the face of seemingly superior technology, of whatever nature, our own weapons would appear to be virtually useless. Therefore, one might be wise to think twice before taking up arms against a UFO or any of its occupants. There's little evidence that they'd do any good whatsoever, and at least some suggestion that they might result in actual harm for the otherwise innocent victims.

BEHIND THE SCENES: After reading about the Hopkinsville, Kentucky case in which the Sutton family shot at ETs, and a few other cases of this type, I became fascinated by what would happen if somebody shot at aliens. I began to review the voluminous UFO literature and collect cases of this type. Before long I found dozens of cases and knew that I needed to put together an article.

I wrote the article, originally titled: "Stop: UFO--Don't Shoot!" and sent if off to the MUFON UFO Journal. The journal had published my articles before, and I thought this was a good one.

To my delight, they accepted it and put it on the cover of their March 1993 issue. However, they also did something that surprised me: a disclaimer. I had never seen a disclaimer on one of their articles before, and I haven't seen one since. The disclaimer was as follows: "MUFON DISCLAIMER: Theme articles such as the above invariably involve a survey of the existing UFO literature, unfortunately the latter varies considerably in terms of authenticity and reliability, dependent upon the original investigator, and his or her relevant sources, all of which are obviously beyond our control. Consequently, MUFON cannot stand behind each and every case as cited. Personal opinions expressed there-in are solely those of the author and should not necessarily be construed as those of the Mutual UFO Network, its Board of Directors or the editors of the Journal."

It was a rather lengthy disclaimer, and though the MUFON UFO Journal regularly presents themed articles and controversial cases, mine is the only one to have received a disclaimer. Oddly, although MUFON distanced itself from the article, they also praised it by publishing the article and giving it the cover.

I received a lot of reaction from the article and was later approached by someone interested in including it in an anthology. Unfortunately that never happened, until being included in this collection, which also has new additional cases that did not appear in the original article. Even as this book was going to press, more cases continued to surface, including several dramatic incidents which occurred to US soldiers during the Vietnam War. In one case, a strange object appeared overhead and despite gunfire from both Vietnamese and US forces, the craft remained unaffected and many of the shells appeared to explode prematurely. Another more dramatic case involved US forces who fired a missile at a UFO only to have the missile "absorbed" into the craft and shot back at them. Likely there are more cases out there. By now, however, the pattern is clear. Shooting at UFOs is not recommended.

Chapter Four
Alien Zoos

Most UFO investigators agree that UFOs are conducting a long-term study of our planet and its inhabitants. UFOs have been seen hovering over military installations, nuclear bases, reservoirs and other sensitive structures. Even more revealing is the fact that they have been seen collecting plants and animals of all different kinds. In addition, research suggests that as many as one in fifty people may have been abducted and given medical examinations aboard a UFO.

If such a study is in fact being conducted, then several questions should be asked. For instance, what is happening to all those "specimens" that have been collected by these aliens? Although people are almost invariably returned after a UFO abduction, plants and animals have literally disappeared from the face of the earth after a close encounter with a UFO. Could it be that the aliens are collecting plants and animals for an alien zoo?

As incredible as it sounds, this may be what is happening. There are several cases on record in which people report having seen extensive collections of plants and animals aboard UFOs.

One interesting case is that of Catherine, an abductee featured in John Mack's book, Abduction. In Christmas of 1990, Catherine was taken aboard a UFO. She was given the standard examination and was then taken to a room where she was shown babies. It was the next room, however, that amazed Catherine the most.

She was led into a room that contained a full-sized, totally natural pine forest. As Catherine says, "I'm confused but it's there. It's in the room, and there's like trees and rocks and dirt and things off to the left. I can see them from where I am."

Catherine was stunned to be inside a forest. It even smelled real. She estimated it to be about the size of a high school gym. There were curving walls going upwards on all sides.

After being taken through the forest, the aliens led Catherine out of the ship and took her back to her home.

Extraterrestrials are not only growing whole forests, but they are also collecting animals of all sorts. One well-known case is that of a Wyoming hunter, Carl Higdon. On October 25, 1974, Higdon was hunting elk along the northern boundary of the Medicine Bow National Forest.

Higdon had been searching for game for several hours when he spotted five elk grazing in a nearby field. He lifted his gun, aimed and pulled the trigger.

To his surprise, the bullet went about halfway, stopped and fell to the ground. Higdon then became aware of an unusual-looking figure standing near him. The figure looked human except he had yellowish skin, a slanted head with thin hair that stood straight up and no visible chin. He was extremely bowlegged, and was dressed in a strange black suit with a wide belt.

Higdon was stunned when the figure invited him aboard a UFO that he only then noticed. Before he realized what was happening, Higdon found himself strapped to a chair inside the UFO. He then felt a sensation of movement. Afterwards he was told that they had traveled 163,000 "light miles." Higdon then saw what appeared to be a futuristic-looking city.

After a short while, Higdon was returned. However, while he was aboard the ship, he noticed that the five elk he had been hunting had also been taken aboard. They had been put into a cubicle in which none of them could move. Higdon was told by the aliens that the elk were needed for breeding purposes.

Another interesting case is that of Denise and Bert Twiggs of Molalla, Oregon. In 1976, the Twiggs experienced a missing-time UFO encounter while driving outside of Rapid City, South Dakota. They explored the event under hypnosis and a typical abduction scenario emerged. The Twiggs, however, worked through the trauma often associated with such encounters. Shortly later, they began having further encounters of a more interactive kind.

They eventually developed a very intimate relationship with aliens from the Andromeda galaxy who call themselves Andromes. Their story is told in their book, Secret Vows: Our Lives with Extraterrestrials.

During their contacts, they experienced many incredible events including several healings of physical ailments. They have also been taken onboard a large mother ship that contains a full complement of nearly all types of earth animals. As the Twiggs say, "One interesting part of the mother ship is the animal reserve. It is a veritable Noah's Ark. Lions, bears, wolves, birds and elephants are to be found there. The majority of these animals are from Earth, although the Andromes have also brought animals from their own and other planets."

The Andromes are not only collecting animals, but also plants. As the Twiggs say, "Equal to their love for animals is their love for nature. The vegetation on the mother ship for the most part seems much like the forests of evergreens here on Earth, specifically reminding us of the Black Hills of South Dakota, although the trees are not as tall. Yet they do have other plants that are not familiar to us, like their fire bush, a three-foot-tall bush in which a red liquid courses through the almost clear branches. From a distance its luminescent qualities and movement make it appear to have a fire dancing across it. There is also a tree in the shape of a giant banana, whose bark resembles something like the shape of a pineapple."

Another case of a perhaps more bizarre nature is that of Katharina, an Oregon-based real-estate broker who has been having UFO encounters all her life. Katharina has been abducted several times, has been examined by the aliens, has been shown hybrid babies, and has been subjected to many other experiences that are typical of onboard UFO experiences. And like many UFO abductees, she has experienced some interference with the United States military, or some faction thereof.

On July 23, 1988, Katharina was taken aboard a UFO where she saw several people, including members of her own family. Several of them were taken to a large area that appeared to be some sort of a zoo. In large glass cages, Katharina was surprised to see a variety of animals, none of which she had ever seen before. As she says, "This huge, dark area we are in looks like a zoo except, instead of cages, they use big glass rooms. They look like displays. I can walk all the way around them...Ooh! I'm looking inside one--I see two gorilla-like Beings and a large cat. The hairy Beings are very tall, and they don't really look like gorillas, but they are all hairy like them. They are asleep."

Katharina was surprised to see that the gorilla-like creature had fallen asleep holding a newspaper, although she had no idea if the creature could actually read. The enclosure did have furniture, including a desk, chairs and books. Katharina also noticed a large cat-like creature. As she says, "There is a cat on the other side of the room. It is white with orange spots, and it is about two to three feet tall. It must weigh over fifty pounds. It was sleeping, but now it is stretching a little and rubbing its face against the wall...I'm walking towards another glass enclosure. The animal in this one appears to be half lion and half reptile. It is lying on its back and its mouth has fallen open because it is sleeping. I'm looking at its mouth and I can see rows of teeth. I know what this animal is because I'm telling the people standing next to me. I sense the animals have been saved from extinction. Someone next to me whispers, 'That is something no one on Earth has ever seen before.' I'm nodding in agreement. I'm amazed at what I'm looking at. These animals are incredible."

Katharina's UFO experiences have involved many screen memories and deceptive camouflages set up by the aliens. She feels, however, that the animals she saw were actually there. As she says, "The animals in the glass enclosures were very real. Again, I did not sense any deception here. Yes, they were unusual, but I felt at that time, and still believe today, that these animals were very rare and were being saved from extinction. Another possibility would be to compare this area to one of our own zoos. It is also interesting that even today I remember the sex of the reptile-lion was female. While I was in the dark and large zoo area, I did not see any aliens, but I was aware that they were monitoring us."

Katharina believes that the zoos are not really for display purposes, but are actually for the animals' own benefit. As she says, "I believe these animals were being helped in some way. Yes, they were captive, but they were healthy and well-cared for. The glass appeared to be one-way viewing, that is, we could see the animals, but the animals could not see us. Somehow, I knew these animals were very special to the aliens and we had to be very quiet when viewing them." In March 1989, Katharina was again taken to the alien zoo. On this occasion, however, she saw only birds. As she says, "I must have passed out and now they brought me to another place. I see cages with birds--the cages are about eight feet square. This is like a zoo, except they have only birds."

Another bizarre case seems to involve genetic experimentation of animals. The case comes from UFO researcher and abductee, Karla Turner, Ph.D. In her book, Into the Fringe, Turner writes about the case of Fred, who had a decidedly unpleasant experience aboard a UFO. Under hypnosis, Fred remembered undergoing some kind of surgical procedure in which fluids from Fred's body were injected into a bizarre creature that was also being operated on aboard the UFO. Fred also saw other strange creatures aboard the UFO. As Fred says, "I feel like they are going [to do] something to me with the animal...They are going [to do] something with me, my blood, my sperm and my genes. They are injecting my fluids into this animal...I was lying down, and they were doing something to the animal...taking something from me and putting it into the animal. Then I remember seeing another animal running around. I can't remember what the animal looked like, but it was bizarre. Seems like the animal is part human, part animal. Like a small child around two years old. The one animal that appears to be human seems to be really hairy...They have the animal next to me. The thing appears to be flat, not like a walking animal."

Fred was intrigued even more by the other animal. As he says, "I can't see it clearly. It doesn't have a shirt on. It has some hair, but not a lot. It seems like it has skin, pink or white, on the top and hair on the bottom. Brown hair. My logic is blocking out a good description...whatever it is, it has hooves, like a cow. I'm not seeing the body too clearly."

As Fred watched, the animal was injected with fluid, and removed from the room. Another woman was brought in and given a similar procedure. Afterwards, Fred was returned to his home. It is Fred's opinion that the aliens are experimenting with crossbreeding. As he says, "They are regenerating from animal to human, from human to animal. Regenerating DNA. I think it has something to do with the immune system. Either they are testing our immune system, or doing something with it. What it is I don't know, but they did implant something into the woman. They seem to be crossbreeding too. Between animal and human."

A more recent case from around 2010 occurred near a small village named Coba, located outside of Tulum on the Yucatan Peninsula. A local Mayan taxi-driver named Cacoch reports that he was walking by a small lake on his way home from work late at night when he saw a very large metallic domed-shaped object hovering over the lake as if searching for something. Frightened, Cacoch hid in the reeds. The UFO began to send a beam of light down. Says Cacoch, "Suddenly the beam fell on an unsuspecting crocodile. It was resting near the bank. The beam lifted the crocodile upward and took it onboard the UFO."

Cacoch says that the crocodile appeared to struggle, but was taken quickly into the craft, which moved away. Two days later, Cacoch was walking in the same area with a friend when the UFO returned and abducted a second crocodile, dumping the body of the first one back in the lake.

Probably the most revealing of these types of cases is that of Betty Andreasson of Massachusetts. On January 26, 1967, Betty Andreasson was taken out of her home and into an alien ship. She was given a painful examination in which she believes she was implanted. She was then placed inside an enclosed chair. When she was taken out, she was led down a tunnel and into a landscape that looked totally unfamiliar and otherworldly. There were strange buildings with window-like openings. It was in one of these strange buildings that Betty saw a large number of very strange creatures.

Crawling along the walls and floor of the one-story building were dozens of one-foot tall creatures with no heads and two eyes located on the ends of stalks that grew from the tops of the lemurs or monkey-like creatures. As Betty says, "There're loads of them. Oh, they're scary! And they've skinny arms and legs and kind of a full body. And their eyes can move every which way, and they can climb just like monkeys. They can climb up quickly and swiftly and down and around and in and out of windows. They are all over the place...they are all around us, everywhere! They are all around and they keep looking at us."

Betty asked the aliens who the creatures were, but they refused to answer.

In 1950, in Westminster, Massachusetts, Betty Andreasson was abducted by aliens from a field behind her home. She was placed inside a large disk filled with jelly-like liquid. As Betty watched through a porthole, the UFO took off and dived into a large body of water. Afterwards, the UFO rose into an underground cavern.

The cavern was completely natural except that there were odd cube-like structures situated in clusters. As Betty approached the cube-like structures, she was shocked to see that they were clear like crystal. And inside each one was a person!

As Betty says, "I'm just moving along beside those odd--I don't know what you would call them--icicles, square icicles or glass things. I don't know. And there is light there...There's people in there, there's some people in there...There's people inside those things. There's some people in there...Inside those glass things, there's some people. But they're not moving."

Betty looked more closely, and she could see that each figure was surrounded by its own distinct scenery. Even more shocking was the wide variety of people represented. Betty saw a Native American, a man from the Renaissance and people from all different times and races. There were also many children. The cubicles were too numerous to count. As Betty says, "There's an Indian in there...There's a whole bunch of people in there...There's people there that are dressed funny and old fashioned...I seen Chinese and just all different peoples there... There's all these different peoples there...There's all these different frozen, or something or other, people there. There's even a dog and a cat and some animals too. There's a whole bunch of stuff there, but I can't see it all."

Betty was then taken to another room that represented a beautiful scene of nature, all in what appeared to be glass. As Betty says, "Oh, everything is just like it's clear glass, like a forest of clear glass. There's leaves and trees and grass and everything, everything. And the birds, they're like thin, thin, thin glass...the only thing is, there's nothing moving. There's even birds flying, but they're not moving. And there's butterflies."

At this point, Betty reached out and touched one of the glass butterflies. To her surprise, it came to life, fluttered around and returned to its frozen state. She reached down to the ground and touched the flowers. The same thing happened. As Betty says, "I'm touching some of the flowers and--Oh! The flowers are beautiful. The color is coming into them and it smells beautiful. Oh. I'm going to touch some leaves. Oh, it's just so beautiful."

Betty was then told by the aliens, "This is for you to remember so mankind will understand."

In 1973, Betty Andreasson was taken to an even more extensive zoo. It was a perfect reproduction of a pond in a forest. In fact, it was so convincing, that when Betty was placed inside the room, she thought she was actually outside. As she says, "I'm in the woods. I don't know how I got here from there, but I'm in the woods...it's so green and beautiful. And there's a pond right there. The water is so clear. I can see fish there. Oh, wow! There's--it's just loaded with fish. Loaded! Loaded!...All sizes of fish in there. And such a small pond too. Oh, and I can see ferns. And it is just so beautiful."

Betty noticed that there was no sun but sort of a strange, even lighting. Shortly later, the pond began draining and Betty saw that it was actually an artificial pond.

Later during the experience, Betty had a chance to communicate with the extraterrestrials. They explained in no uncertain terms that their zoos are actually saving the species on our planet from total extinction. As Betty says, "He says that they are the caretakers of nature and natural forms--The Watchers. They love mankind. They love the planet Earth and they have been caring for it and Man since Man's beginning. They watch the spirit in all things. Man is destroying much of nature...They are curious about the emotions of mankind...He's saying that they have collected the seed of Man, male and female. And that they have been collecting every species and every gender of plant for hundreds of years so that nothing will be lost when the last shall come."

There are many other cases of this kind, but the general pattern is clear. The cases fall into two main types. The first type is a simple collection of genetic material and live specimens. The second type seems to involve genetic experimentation with exotic, unknown creatures.

Why are the aliens collecting these specimens and creating new ones? What do these stories tell us about our future? Are the aliens predicting worldwide disasters and the destruction of all life on planet Earth? Are they collecting species like a sort of futuristic Noah's ark? Are they just performing bizarre genetic experiments for reasons of their own?

Some obvious conclusions can be easily drawn from these types of cases. Evidently, the aliens feel that we are going to destroy ourselves and are only trying to protect humanity from total extinction. Our zoos on Earth are primarily used for display. The alien zoos, however, are much more akin to wildlife reserves. Humans have stood by and done nothing while species after species have been rendered extinct. The aliens, however, have obviously taken action. Thanks to the aliens, many creatures thought to be extinct may actually have been saved. And those that are in danger of extinction may still be saved. Including us.

BEHIND THE SCENES: This article was originally inspired by the Betty Andreasson case. When I discovered other cases, I was astounded by their similarity, and so this article was born. It was originally published in UFO Encounters Magazine (Volume 2, #6, 1995), which had previously published several of my other articles. Like most articles, it enjoyed a brief life and was quickly replaced by the next issue of the magazine never to be seen again. A few years later I was surfing the internet and found that my article had been lifted from the internet and placed on a website in my name. The entire website was just the one article. I have no idea who put it up there, and it eventually was taken down. It was the first time that something I wrote was used without my knowledge or consent. But it wouldn't be the last.

Chapter Five
UFOs over Graveyards

Graveyards and cemeteries are places usually associated with ghosts. However, several cases are now in record in which UFOs have shown an undue interest in graveyards. The question is, why? What interest could UFOs have in something so macabre as a cemetery?

These types of cases are somewhat rare, but they continue to turn up, and have been confounding leading UFO investigators for years. These are not cases of so-called "spook-lights," but accounts of apparent metallic spacecraft. Let us examine a few cases and see for ourselves.

On the evening of May 7, 1967, fourteen-year-old Ricky Banyard was walking to his home in Edmonton, Alberta, Canada, when he observed a "strange beam of light" emitted from an unknown object in the sky. He quickly ran to the home of his friend, Glenn Coate, and the two boys watched the object through binoculars. They said it "looked like two bowls joined together at the rims, and it hovered, making a whistling noise." It would periodically send powerful beams of light to the ground.

At around 2:00 AM, Glenn became tired and went to bed while Ricky went outside and hid under some trees to watch the object. The next time the object emitted a beam of light, he followed it to the ground and was shocked to realize that it was shining directly on the Mount Pleasant Cemetery across the street from his home. According to the report on the case: "The light beam extended down, striking the ground and making a white, bright, rectangular area on the ground."

Ricky eventually tried to get closer. However as soon as he stepped out from under the trees the beam of light retracted, the lights on the object went out, and the object departed with a "noise like a jet starting up," followed up with several "bangs."

The most interesting aspect of this case was revealed by an inspection of the cemetery the next day. As the report reads: "...an inspection of the cemetery yielded several unexplained rectangular black streaks on the sand and gravel paths leaving among the graves. Rocks and pebbles seemed to be charred, but none of the grassy area or trees appeared to have been harmed.

"Joseph LaForge, the cemetery foreman, could not explain the marks, but suggested that a grader had gone over the roads on Saturday and may have exposed some of the cinder base under the gravel. He then pointed to two other large marks and said, 'I don't know about them--they look pretty unusual.' He couldn't account for the black marks on the stones and explained that no oil is used on the cemetery roads."

A second case occurred in June 8, 2011 over an Illinois graveyard. A man was in his home when his dog started acting oddly. "She was overly restless and barking," says the man. "She kept barking toward the south."

He decided to take the dog outside. As the dog began "racing around," he looked around searching for whatever was upsetting his dog. Looking up, he saw a bright white light with "red lights all around it."

Says the witness, "It was just hovering above the graveyard at the end of our street."

The witness was shocked, because only a few weeks earlier he had seen the same object hovering over the neighborhood. He ran inside and retrieved a camera and another family member. Says the witness, "We stood there and watched it for a few minutes, and it took off to the southeast, very slow moving...It was pretty high up off the ground, but I can't say for sure how high it was. With my dog still being nutty, I brought her in and locked the doors."

Another even stranger case occurred early 1967. The witness is the anonymous owner of a funeral home. The whole ordeal began when the owner's son ran inside and reported that a "flying saucer" was hovering right over the funeral parlor. The owner says that she assumed her son was imagining things and didn't investigate.

Several days later a man was visiting the grave of a deceased friend when he ran inside and told the owner of the funeral parlor that a "disk-shaped, metallic appearing object" was hovering directly over the building. Suddenly remembering her son's earlier report, she ran outside to see, but by then the object was gone.

However she was left thoroughly shaken by the event, and eventually made an official report to the Aerial Phenomena Research Organization (APRO) headed by Jim and Coral Lorenzen. She agreed to report her case only on the condition that the name and location be kept confidential.

A truly alarming case from Leominster, Massachusetts, was originally investigated by pioneering UFO researcher J. Allen Hynek. It began on March 8, 1967 when a young couple (a painter and a hairdresser) went out for a drive to look at the newly fallen snow. It was around 1:00 AM on a clear night and they were passing a small cemetery outside of Leominster.

Both noticed that the cemetery was strangely shrouded in fog, even though it was clear everywhere else. Then they spotted a strange light directly over the cemetery, and their initial reaction was that there must be a fire in the cemetery and the fog was actually smoke. They took a closer look, and at this point things went from strange to bizarre.

As the investigator's report says: "He turned the car around again and put his windows down and drove off the road broadside to the cemetery and to the light...he got out of his car, shut the door and started to point to the object. Simultaneously several events occurred: the automobile lights, radio and engine ceased functioning; he felt an electrical shock, and his body became numb and immobilized; the arm he was point with was pulled up against the roof of the car and with such a force that it left an imprint in the ice and snow...Mr. W. could not move a muscle, although he could hear, and his mind seemed to be functioning normally. Then the lights and radio came back on, and the object which had been rocking back and forth emitted a humming sound and accelerated upward and out of sight above the fog patch."

The two witnesses were left thoroughly frightened by the event. As one said, "Nothing I have ever seen compares with this object."

With nearly a dozen books and hundreds of cases to his credit, Raymond Fowler has made a lasting contribution to the UFO field. It should come as no surprise that he was among the first to notice a connection between UFOs and graveyards. According to Fowler, approximately twenty-three percent of his cases took place over rural fields, a portion of which were actually cemeteries. Writes Fowler, "I had no idea then that cemeteries...would figure in future UFO investigations."

In the AM hours of October 6, 1964, Robert Cousy and his friend William Chase drove through the country outside of Haverhill, Massachusetts. Chase spotted the object first: a domed disk hovering above the trees next to a graveyard.

Soucey put his car in reverse and backed up until they could see the object closely. At this point it was only 150 feet away. According to Soucey, "It looked like a half ball on a flat plate. We both stared at it for about twenty seconds and then got out of there real fast. No one else was around and we were plenty scared."

In fact, the two men were so upset by what they saw that they drove straight to the police station. Seeing that the two men were sincerely frightened, the police sent a car to the scene of the sighting. But by then the object was gone.

A rare case involving humanoids occurred on October 9, 1954 at a cemetery in Pournay-La-Chetive in France. Four children ranging in age from five to sixteen years old were roller-skating by the cemetery near their homes when they encountered a UFO. It hovered directly over the graveyard and was described as round, luminous and about three meters in diameter.

All four witnesses watched in shock as a short figure appeared. It was dressed in black, with large eyes and hair on its face. It shone a "blinding light" at them and spoke in an "unknown language." The four young witnesses fled in terror, but turned around in time to see the object take off and fly away."

A particularly alarming case was investigated by Eugene H. Frison, the MUFON Provincial Director for Nova Scotia, Canada. In this case a paperboy had taken a shortcut through the local cemetery to deliver papers. Once inside the cemetery grounds he noticed an increase in wind and a strange whining sound, followed by a sudden rush of heat. On his right, three feet away, he observed a triangular-shaped object about nine feet tall and five feet wide, hover and move quickly by him and out of view.

Apparently the paperboy had surprised the UFO after it had landed in the cemetery. The witness did not observe anything else unusual. However immediately following the incident, he suffered raised blisters across his chest and face. The blisters stung and burned if picked, but disappeared after a few days.

On November 4, 1957, yet another encounter occurred which indicates that UFOs show a strong interest in graveyards. At 3:12 AM that morning, Patrolman Joseph Lukasek, Patrolman Clifford Schau, and Fireman Robert Volt of Elmwood, Illinois were in their squad car investigating a store which had an open window. Suddenly one of them spotted a strange bright red-orange, egg-shaped object hovering 250 feet in the air, directly over the Elmwood Cemetery.

They turned the spotlight on the object and radioed Officer Daniel DeGiovanni at the Elmwood Police Station that they were observing an "unknown object." At that instant, the headlights and spotlight dimmed and flickered repeatedly.

The object appeared to be "folding into itself." But when they turned on the spotlight, it "puffed out," shot up 200 feet and took off. The officers chased after the object in their car, but hit a dead-end street. Still they were able to watch the object "fold inward from the bottom" and disappear.

Back at the Elmwood Park Police Station, officer DeGiovanni ran outside just in time to observe the object shoot across town and disappear.

Many other cases are on record. One evening in December 1966, Rob McKinnon (a rest area operator) observed a bright beam of light "hanging absolutely motionless in the air, maybe 100 feet up." McKinnon called his family and they all observed the light descend over the nearby burial ground.

McKinnon and his family observed that the huts containing the bodies were brightly lit by the beams. Said McKinnon, "We definitely had a feeling

87

it was interested in this place...there definitely was something strange happening there over the cemetery that night."

In 1989, Nelson Oliveira, the local grave-digger for the Aracariguama Cemetery outside of Sao Paolo, Brazil, experienced a dramatic graveyard encounter. According to an interview with South American ufologist Hermes de Fonseca, Oliveira observed a classic metallic flying saucer which he described as "an upside-down hat" made of aluminum. Oliviera observed the object hover low over the cemetery for several minutes before quickly flying away.

In an interview with journalist Gerri Miller, the famous rock-star Rob Zombie says that in 1973 he was leaving a Halloween party when he saw a UFO hovering over the cemetery next to his grade school. "That was pretty freaky," said Zombie.

On June 16, 2011, a lady was driving along Route 29 in Chillicothe, Illinois when her radio became filled with static. To the side of the road she instantly noticed "two very large, orange lights" hovering over the local cemetery. She saw other cars pulling over to observe the lights. She also pulled over and quickly called her brother and told him to get to the cemetery and look at the UFOs.

"I watched them for the next few minutes," says the witness. "They just stayed above the cemetery, not moving."

The objects appeared to be "teardrop-shaped or cone-shaped, the base being the largest part, and glowing an extremely bright orange." A dozen orange spikes of light pointed downward toward the cemetery. After a few moments, the lights started to dim and move away. The witness quickly hopped back in her car and followed them. Moments later, a helicopter appeared and also began to chase the lights. Both quickly moved out of view.

A few minutes later, her brother (who was about six blocks away) called to say that he had just seen one of the lights dart by, followed by the helicopter. Says the sister, "We weren't able to make much sense of it, but definitely believe that the helicopter was following in their direction." The witness was so impressed by her sighting that she reported it officially to MUFON.

Researcher Scott Corrales reports on a case which occurred on April 5, 1996 in Paraiba, Brazil. Maria Jose and her son were driving when they saw a UFO hovering over the local cemetery. At that moment, the object sped directly toward them, moving just above the car's roof. Maria Jose was so frightened by the encounter that she had to be hospitalized.

Another UFO-graveyard case uncovered by Scott Corrales occurred on October 23, 1977 to Ana Rumin and Manuel Fernandez in Gerena, Spain. The two witnesses were walking home when they noticed that a strange reddish glow was rising up from the cemetery grounds not far from where they were walking. Deciding to investigate, they went to the home of Ruperto Munoz, which overlooked the cemetery.

Rumin and Fernandez climbed to the roof, joined by Munoz and his wife, and all four saw that the reddish glow was coming from a red circular object which was already heading off into the distance, occasionally blinking from red to green.

On July 15, 1996, a young man described by police as a "sensible sort of lad and genuine" was walking by a cemetery in Chesire, England on his way home when he saw a yellow light hovering at tree top level over the cemetery. The object made a high-pitched noise "like cats wailing" and suddenly began to fire beams of light at the railway line.

As the young man left the scene, the object began to follow him. He fled the area and returning home, told his father what he had seen. They both returned to the scene and found the four railway sleepers still smoldering, one with a four-inch hole burnt through it. They contacted police who arrived in time to see the smoldering wood. The officer could find no evidence of accelerants to start the fire and said, "It does look rather odd."

Perhaps the most complex and chilling of all UFO-graveyard encounters, this next case-- investigated by veteran journalist Bob Teets-- involves dozens of witnesses, all of whom have regularly seen UFOs hovering over a group of cemeteries located in Elk Garden, West Virginia.

The sightings seem to concentrate over a particular area called Nethken Hill. However, the only thing on the hill is a small church surrounded by cemeteries including the Nethken Cemetery, the Kalbaugh Cemetery, and the Dean Memorial Cemetery. The sightings began in the early 1960s and seem to be ongoing.

The Jones family is only one of many families in this small town that have seen UFOs over the cemeteries. In April of 1968 two members of the family were driving by the graveyard when they saw a bright ball of light hovering overhead. Both watched as the 100-foot orange sphere moved brazenly over their vehicle. As it got closer, they saw a metallic structure to the object and heard a high-pitched buzzing noise.

Overcome with fear, they sped away. The object, however, followed them home, hovering above their car. The terrified couple darted into the family home and woke up relatives, who came outside and also saw the object, which began to dart from place to place, and then left.

Another family who has seen objects over the local graveyards are the Kalbaughs, who actually have their own family cemetery. Says Amie Kalbaugh, "We'd see lights all during the late 1960s and early '70s going back and forth around the church area. I never wanted to see them, but I did...We would watch the lights and go through a process of elimination, 'not a plane, not a helicopter,' and so forth, and try to figure out what they were...I always thought we heard a high-pitched sound, and then we would look out the window. The lights were always white."

Amie's sister, Vickie, also remembers the sightings. "I saw a silvery white, elliptical-shaped thing in the sky," says Vickie. "I was thinking, 'That's not an airplane or helicopter.' Your mind plays tricks on you when you're frightened, and I remember always being afraid...After these sightings we were always so afraid."

Yet another member of the family, Clark Kalbaugh, reports his own encounter in mid-July 1970. "I was looking out the window toward Nethken Hill Cemetery," says Clark, "when I saw an object moving in the sky over the cemetery...within a flash, it's right over the house! I'm looking directly up at the bottom of this object, which is possibly cigar-shaped to elliptical, somewhere in-between. A lot of bright lights on the bottom, very bright--ten to fifteen bright lights. As quickly as it's there, bam! It's gone again. Then I see the lights toward Elk Garden, on Nethken Hill Cemetery again."

Yet another witness to the sightings is local resident and mail-carrier Dixon Ridder. With his residence only one mile north of the graveyard, Dixon had an excellent view of the area. On one occasion Dixon saw "...a brilliant white light with a sharp outline on its edge...it was about five feet in diameter, and was just a few feet back from the church. All of a sudden, it went to the back of the church, then went across the road to that Dean Monument over there, where, just like you turn a light out, it vanished."

The sightings became so frequent over the graveyard that residents would sometimes stake out the area just to see a UFO. Usually nothing happened, but on one occasion, three people witnessed the granddaddy of UFO-graveyard encounters.

On October 8, 1967, Reverend Harley DeLeurere and two other residents decided to go UFO hunting at the graveyards. They hiked to within a quarter mile of the area and waited to see what would happen. After two hours they were startled by a bright flash of light. Seconds later, they saw a classic flying saucer. As one witness described, "...something like a big turtle with lights on it appeared level with the top of the house...it wasn't more than six feet off the ground, and it had three or four recessed lights on it that shined toward the graveyard and down on the ground too."

As the three men watched, the object hovered low over each of the graveyards, shining down powerful beams of light as if searching for something. They then noticed a chilling detail. The object stopped and targeted a particular gravesite with its beam of light. The only thing unusual about this gravesite was that it was very recent--only a day old. In fact, the funeral had just been held earlier that day.

After several minutes of hovering over the gravesite and shining down beams of light, the object "disappeared." The three men inspected the area, but nothing seemed to be disturbed. Said one witness, "We thought for sure we'd see something, but when we got there, there wasn't anything there."

Reverend DeLeurere recommended that the body be exhumed and examined for "signs of disturbance." However nothing was ever done. The witnesses were convinced that the UFO was showing a definite interest in the new grave. It was a pattern they would observe on many occasions. Said one witness: "It seemed like every time there was a new grave, within the next couple of nights, people would see lights up there."

With more than a dozen cases on record occurring across the world, it becomes difficult to deny that UFOs are showing an expressed interest in graveyards. But why would aliens be interested in graveyards? This next case may provide an answer, though perhaps not a very pleasant one.

In March of 1992, Pennsylvania teacher, James L. Walden experienced his first fully conscious encounter with extraterrestrials. Later under hypnosis, Walden would recall a lifetime of alien encounters, beginning with his birth.

According to his regression, he was actually implanted in his mother's womb by the aliens. His DNA, however, has a different source. As he says under hypnosis, "I am a composite of other people and beings. Some parts of me came from humans; others came from aliens. I'm not unique. I am composed of part of all the people who were used to create me!"

In other words, Walden is saying that his embryo was created from genes harvested from a number of different people. He says, "I saw the alien beings harvesting brain cells from dying human bodies, then combining the cells to make my embryo...I see the corpses of two men and one woman. When they died, the aliens--who cannot be seen by humans--are present, and they retrieve tissue samples to use in creating me...the woman's corpse was the most vivid. I didn't recognize her."

As can be seen, aliens have shown a strong interest in graveyards. But again, the question is why? What is it about graveyards that ETs find so attractive? Could it be simple curiosity, or is there another explanation?

UFO researchers Jim and Coral Lorenzen had their own speculations. They write: "The Edmonton cemetery reports is one of many involving strange objects near cemeteries or old burial grounds. When the two reports--the object over the funeral home, and the object over the cemetery--are taken alone, they don't make much sense; they just give one a kind of queasy feeling about possible supernatural phenomena. However, when considered in context with hundreds of sightings of objects following cars, especially at night, a faint connection is possible.

"UFOs have been following cars at night for years. At night, cars have their headlights on. Whether or not curiosity is the motivation for these antics, we cannot tell, but if intelligent beings are behind these visits, then they also might well be curious about a long line of cars driving in the daytime with their lights on when no lights are needed--the typical behavior of funeral processions. If intelligent beings in a hovering craft became curious about such an event, they then might indeed try to find out the purpose of such a procession. They could note that a box was removed and buried in the ground. So they might try to discern what a funeral home is, and ultimately, a cemetery."

That the aliens are intensely curious in human affairs is pretty obvious. It could very well be that the above cases show only that UFOs are studying yet another aspect of human society.

Well-known researcher Scott Corrales's study of these types of cases reveals other possible reasons. He speculates that "the UFOs were engaged in the business of retrieving alien implants..." He asks, "Why are the UFOs interested in our final resting places? What could they stand to gain from such pursuits? Trying to ascribe reason to an utterly unreasonable phenomenon leads us to consider that 'alien scientists' can glean important biological information from the deceased, or as suggested in the West Virginia scenario, we are witnessing a clean-up operation aimed at removing implants left in the bodies of long-time abductees?"

There is always the possibility that the aliens are a little more than just curious. Could it be that they are, in fact, actively engaged in the systematic exhumation and exploitation of human corpses? After all, the only things of any interest in graveyards are the bodies. Why else would UFOs shine a beam of light down on a freshly dug grave? Although this is pure speculation, the UFOs' interest in graveyards is not.

The Dean Memorial Cemetery and Walden cases strengthen the theory that at least some aliens may be robbing graves for the express purpose of obtaining genetic material. And if one wanted to obtain DNA from a certain person with the least possible disturbance, then waiting until the person actually died makes some sense. Interestingly, genetic material remains alive for a period of days following biological death. This would explain why the UFOs over Dean Memorial Cemetery not only targeted the new graves, but reportedly appeared every time there had been a new grave dug.

Also consider the following report from respected UFO researchers, Raymond Fowler and Walter Webb. Writes Fowler, "One afternoon [Summer 1964], Walter phones to say that he had received a tip concerning an alleged UFO landing near a cemetery at Lawrence, Massachusetts. Would I be willing to assist in his investigations? I excitedly agreed."

That evening they interviewed a group of children who claimed to have seen an object land next to the cemetery. They explored the graveyard, but were unable to find anything unusual. Then came the shocking news. As Fowler writes, "A few days later, a fellow employee informed me that there had been a grave robbery in this same cemetery that very week, and the Lawrence Police had staked it out! What would we have said if the police caught us creeping from tombstone to tombstone?"

Further evidence supporting the theory of alien grave-robbers comes from researcher Bill Knell. Following a rash of animal mutilations, rumors began to circulate among the UFO community that there were also cases of human mutilations. Knell tracked down one such rumor to a medical examiner in Westchester County, New York, who informed him that several morgues in the area had been "hit" and "fresh human cadavers" were mutilated in the same style as the well-known cattle mutilations.

In this case, the damage included partial removal of the face, and total removal of the eyes, thyroid, stomach, and genitals. Knell was informed

97

by the anonymous medical examiner that the morgues in question quickly enacted a cover-up, and that the public was never told the truth.

If these speculations are true, an interesting experiment might be to stake out cemeteries immediately following the placement of any new coffins with human remains. Even more interesting would be a study of the already targeted gravesites. In other words, is there any evidence that the body was disturbed? Whose grave is it, and why would the aliens be interested in them? Are the individuals in the graves genetically unique or unusual in any way? Have they had any prior UFO experiences? Are the gravesites of recently deceased UFO abductees likely to cause an encounter?

These, of course, are mysteries that remain to be solved.

BEHIND THE SCENES: I got the idea for this article after picking up Bob Teets' book, West Virginia UFOs, and reading about the Dean Memorial Cemetery Case. By coincidence, I had just read about the J. Allen Hynek case. I instantly recalled that Fowler and the Lorenzens had investigated these types of cases. And so I began to review the literature and collect the cases. It didn't take long to gather enough cases to build a very strong case that UFOs and graveyards have a strange connection. Given that extraterrestrials are very interested in genetics, it seems quite possible that they are stealing genetic material from graves.

I put together an article and sent it off to Fate Magazine. To my disappointment, they rejected it.

Certainly this was not the first time they had returned one of my submissions. In fact, I sent them many articles before they finally began to accept them. Lately, however, they had been accepting my articles. I thought this was a good one, exactly the type of article they often publish, and it certainly took quite a bit of research. I was puzzled why they had rejected it.

I got my answer when the next issue arrived in the mail. Inside the issue was an excellent article by esteemed researcher, Scott Corrales. The article was called, "Strange Places: UFOs and Cemeteries." The article was eerily similar to mine. Both articles were built around the Dean Memorial Cemetery Case, though each of us managed to find different cases to support the UFO-graveyard connection. Obviously Fate couldn't publish two such similar articles. Corrales had beaten me to the punch!

I updated my article to include a few quotes from (and give credit to!) Corrales' article and sent it off to the MUFON UFO Journal. It was published in the June 2002 issue as the lead article. The above version has been updated again, with still more additional cases.

Chapter Six
They Walk Among Us

Ever since the modern age of UFOs began in the late 1940s, humanity's relationship with extraterrestrials has been growing and evolving. What first began with distant sightings of anomalous craft have now become full-blown abductions. However, as time moves on, our relationship with UFOs continues to change. People are now reporting cases of a decidedly alarming nature.

For the most part, extraterrestrials seem to have kept out of human affairs. Abductions are done covertly, and sightings over large industrial centers are relatively rare. However, recently there have been several reports of a new type of encounter. In these cases, people are not taken aboard a UFO. Nor do they have a visitation in which an alien appears in their home. Rather, in these cases, people are encountering aliens in public places, in broad daylight!

Are aliens actually able to infiltrate our society and walk among us undetected? As crazy as this sounds, this is exactly what seems to be happening. Let us examine a few cases.

Whitley Strieber's book, Communion, took the world by storm and spent months on the New York Times bestseller list. In late January 1987 in New York City, senior editor of Morrow Books, Bruce Lee and his wife were in a bookstore admiring a new display of Strieber's book when something very strange happened.

"I noticed a couple come into the store," explains Lee, "and head directly for Communion. I mean, it was just, you just see them come in--they didn't know where the book was, you couldn't see it from the street--and they come in and headed back for where that rack was. Most unusual if you see what I mean...they were short...and they were all wrapped up. Long scarves, wool hats that you pull down, and they picked up a copy of the book, and they started thumbing through it...and it was obvious that they were speed-reading it too. And they would say, 'Oh, he's got it wrong, he's got that wrong.'"

Because he was personally involved in publishing the book, Lee approached the couple an asked them what was wrong with the book. "I think it was the woman that looked up," says Lee. "She was wearing those big sort of sunglasses that the girls keep up in their hair. And they really sort of hide the face. But by God behind those dark glasses there was a goddamn big pair of eyes. And I mean to say it was a big pair of eyes. And they were shaped liked almonds. You know how when you meet somebody the first time you can frequently get an immediate reaction? The hackles on the back of my neck just went up. I got to feeling that I was in eyeball contact with somebody who did not like me at all. In fact, I got the impression that I was not wanted around there...I went over and got my wife and got the hell out of there. I was almost shaking. I said, 'Did you see that couple?' and my wife said, 'Sure I saw that couple.' And I said, 'Well, they don't look like goddamn people!' And she said, 'Well, you're crazy.'...it was really a very intense shock."

Lee says that virtually no skin was visible on the figures. As he says, "[They were] short...they were wearing boots and it was sort of hard with those hats on, to tell what was there, underneath all the clothing. And of course, you couldn't see the hands, because they were in gloves."

What most amazed Lee, however was the speed at which the two "people" were able to read. "You do know when somebody's reading something and comprehending it," says Lee, "and these pages were turning very, very fast."

As unbelievable as it sounds, Mr. Lee and his wife both witnessed what appeared to be extraterrestrials who were able to disguise themselves enough to pass for human, at least in New York City.

Strieber says of Lee's encounter: "Mr. Lee feels that the event has brought him nothing but unwelcome exposure...This appearance was, I believe, as close to public and physical confirmation of their existence as the visitors have yet come."

A second bizarre case of an alien in a public place occurred in December 1984 to an anonymous woman. According to her own account, she and two co-workers had just closed the office at around 11:00 PM and were walking along the street to a small market. "Just as I reached the corner," says the woman, "three globes of red light, about the size and shape of eggs, suddenly appeared in a circle around me. They floated around me rapidly, at knee height...I am a large woman and sensitive to pranks, so I looked around to see if somebody was playing a joke on me. I thought maybe Tim or Harry [her co-workers] was using some sort of red flashlight to confused and frighten me. I looked up and saw both of them standing across the street and called out to them, 'What are you doing?' Both of them stared back at me in amazement."

Stunned and amazed, the woman headed home but stopped at a nearby deli. This is when things went from strange to bizarre. Only minutes earlier she had seen the strange lights. And then, as she says, "All the counter guys at the deli know me; I go there all the time, but that night there was a new guy I'd never seen before. He was very tall--at least six feet three or four. His appearance was striking: he looked like he may have been a combination of African, Oriental and Nordic blood. His skin was very pale with a yellowish cast, and his hair was Negroid, with tight, kinky curls, except that it was the color of wheat. He had a broad mouth and very large, remarkable eyes, the color of gold coins, almond-shaped and slanted. He was dressed in the white uniform of a deli man.

"I put the milk on the counter and asked for my brand of cigarettes. I mentioned that he must be new there because I knew everybody else, and he smiled gently and looked into my eyes with a searching gaze. When he gave me my change, I noticed that his hands were very smooth and his fingers were very long. He seemed to be looking beyond me into the snowy night when he said, 'It doesn't happen very often, but when it does, it can be very scary.'"

The witness was confused by the remark, and thought he perhaps meant the snow. But the man looked at her as if to say, "Don't you know what I mean?"

The woman left the store and tried to put the experience behind her. However, it was not over yet. The next day at work, her co-workers Tim and Harry cornered her, demanding to know, "What were those red lights around you last night?"

One of them described it as looking like a ribbon of fire spiraling around her body. The lady could only shrug and admit her own puzzlement. She did, however, go visit the deli and see if the strange new employee had happened to see anything. When she went there, however, there was no sign of the strange-looking man. Not only was he not there, the regular employees vehemently denied that there was ever any new employee. They said flatly, "There ain't no new guy." Despite her protests, the deli workers insisted that not only was there no new employee, neither of them remembered her coming into the deli the night before!

And so the lady was left with the possibility that she had encountered an alien in a very unlikely place.

Lisa Arrons of Fort Myers, Florida reports yet another bizarre experience involving aliens walking among us. One evening in the mid-1990s, she was driving home when she spotted a metallic disk. Shortly later, she experienced about one hour of missing time and suddenly found herself pulling into a gas-station. She was understandably confused and as she went to pay for her gas, she was wondering about what had just happened to her.

At this point things went from bizarre to incredible. "When I walked back to my car," said Arrons, "a man was standing there--leaning on the trunk. This is embarrassing...He was gorgeous! Beautiful blue eyes! He spoke. I stopped and stared at him. He smiled. I stuttered and couldn't believe my eyes when I offered him a ride. I have never, ever done such a crazy thing before, but he was different. Somehow I couldn't stop myself. I took him to my house."

Lisa couldn't understand her behavior, as she was not in the habit of picking up men, no matter how beautiful they might be. But for some reason, she couldn't control her impulses. Before she knew it, they were in her bedroom having sex. Again things went from incredible to downright unbelievable. Says Lisa, "Later that night I felt him get up from the bed. The night-light in my bedroom was on and I could see him standing naked next to a full-length mirror. This next second is frozen in my mind. His reflection in the mirror was unreal. What I saw was the image of a small dark creature with a big head and huge eyes. I sat up in bed. He moved into the bathroom and out of sight. When I finally looked in the bathroom, he was gone, and there is no window in the bathroom. I know this sounds crazy..."

Another case of an alien in a public case occurred to Debbie Jordan, the central witness in Budd Hopkins' landmark book, Intruders. She has had the full range of UFO experiences, ranging from early childhood encounters to full-blown missing time abductions. One of her encounters, however, shows how easily it might be for aliens to walk among us.

On July 4, 1975, Debbie and a few friends went camping in Rough River State Park in Kentucky. She and her friends were talking on the CB radio to some guys. Then the experience became suddenly strange. Says Debbie, "They wanted to come and see us, and I told them if they could find us they would be welcome."

As if on cue, the guys showed up, however, as Debbie says, "It sort of didn't make any sense...We could never figure out how they found us in the first place, either, because when we were talking to them on the CB we never told them how to get where we were. There weren't even any names for the roads around there, so I couldn't have explained it even if I wanted to. They just showed up, as I remembered, in a kind of clunky old car with hardly any lights on it."

Debbie and her friends saw what appeared to be four normal-looking young men. They were dressed in blue shirts and all looked very similar. Only one of them did any talking, although they stayed in the cabin for hours. The one who appeared to be the "leader" was, according to Debbie, "...real cute...He had a round face and blue eyes, real light, light brown, light blond hair...curly down to his collar."

The four men simply sat with the ladies for about four hours. At the time, they seemed normal. However, in retrospect, Debbie remembers several strange details. First of all was that only one of them ever spoke. "The other two guys just sort of stood there," says Debbie. "One stood by the door. I don't think they ever said anything at all."

Debbie's friend, Sam, agreed and said that the two guys stood "sort of like guards while the blond guy ran things."

Another strange detail that turned up later was not only the fact that the guys were able to find them, but how they approached. Their car, said Debbie, "glided along without bouncing...its light was very steady and didn't go up and down as it went over the bumps." This detail was bothersome because it was a dirt road, and very bumpy.

Debbie admitted also to being unreasonably obsessed with the blond guy. She said that he "smiled with his eyes." Budd Hopkins writes, "It was a phrase I'd heard before in other UFO cases."

But probably the strangest detail was when Debbie first took the strange visitors into their cabin. It was very late, and she was afraid of waking everyone up. When she entered, she was confronted with a sight so bizarre, she could hardly understand it. As she says, "I was sure some of them would have been in bed, since it was late, but they were all up, just sitting there and standing, and the TV wasn't even on...They were just still, you know, not moving, like they were hardly awake, and not saying anything. And my head started to feel funny, between my eyes, and then the blond guy spoke and everyone kind of came to life, and began to move and talk. It was really weird, like they had been asleep or something."

This detail is recognized by many UFO researchers. Writes Hopkins, "As we have seen, one of the basic patterns in UFO abductions, part of the modus operandi, is the ability the abductors have to 'shut people off,' as it were, for as long as the particular operation lasts...This state of 'suspended animation' has been reported by UFO investigators in widely differing situations and with varying numbers of abductees involved."

Eventually the strange visitors left the cabin, and everyone returned to sleep. It wasn't until much later that Debbie realized that there were many unexplained events that occurred that evening. Later, Debbie would experience an astonishing sequel to this event.

In 1983, Debbie Jordan had yet another encounter with what may have been an extraterrestrial masquerading as a human. She had not yet undergone regressive hypnosis to recall her experience, but was quite aware that something strange was going on. She had had several close-up sightings, some events involving missing time, and other clues pointing to her involvement with the UFO phenomenon.

On the night in question, she had recently contacted Budd Hopkins to discuss her experiences, and was understandably upset and confused by the bizarre turn of events. She was returning from visiting Hopkins in New York City and was taking a bus ride home. Somewhere in Pennsylvania, a very strange passenger got onboard.

Debbie was trying to keep her seat to herself when, as she says, "Suddenly I felt very strange. This prickly sensation washed over me and I got the distinct feeling someone was boarding the bus that I needed to see. I peeked up over the back of the seat in front of me and what I saw nearly took my breath away. There stood the most beautiful man I have ever seen. And he was looking directly at me as he walked up the steps to the bus! It was as if he knew I was there before he even got on the bus. He was about six-feet-four, medium build, yet slim. He had shoulder-length, wavy, medium blond hair, and the most perfectly structured face I have ever seen."

The strange man eventually sat down next to Debbie, and so began the strangest bus ride of her life. As they talked she noticed many strange details about the man. "I noticed that his voice was very soft and smooth," she says, "and he seemed to be speaking with some kind of sing-song accent. It was very slight. So slight, in fact, that I first thought he was faking it for my benefit. I asked him where he was from...he said he was from 'near Sweden.' That didn't make much sense. It didn't sound like a Swedish accent to me."

Another strange detail, says Debbie, "I noticed after a while that he never seemed to show any signs of beard growth, despite the fact that we were together on the bus for more than 17 hours. I also noticed that every time he touched me, however lightly, on the arm or the face, his touch was exceptionally warm and I could feel the warmth flow through my whole body, relaxing and calming me. I didn't realize at the time how unusual any of this was."

At the end of the bus ride, the two of them went to a fast-food restaurant. Again Debbie noticed more unusual behavior. As she says, "When we started to order, [he] turned to me and asked me what the difference was between bacon and sausage. Then he asked me what he should eat. I told him what the difference was between those two foods and told him that they were both good by me. He proceeded to order just about one of everything on the menu. When he saw how small the orange-juice containers were, he complained loudly, and then ordered four of them. The girls waiting on us looked at him as if he were some kind of green-haired alien. I was kind of embarrassed by how he was acting..."

Debbie then thought how much she liked this guy, and couldn't live without him, but might not ever see him again. At that moment, he turned to her and said, "Don't worry, we'll see each other again."

Another strange event occurred shortly later. "We decided to walk to the bush station. We passed a group of people sitting on the benches...They absolutely stared a hole through us as we walked by. I'd bet we were a sight, him so tall and me so short, but the look we got from them was even stranger than just them noticing our different heights. They actually looked totally dumbstruck. I was talking to [him] when I noticed them. It was almost as if I were talking to myself and they thought I was some kind of nut."

The strangeness just kept coming. When Debbie went to the restroom, he started to follow her in, apparently not realizing that men weren't allowed in the women's bathroom. He didn't understand the concept of nausea or vomiting and expressed total fascination when presented with a Pepto-Bismol pill. He also seemed delighted by the colorful newspapers and insisted that Debbie buy him one.

All the strange details came together to make Debbie wonder, who was this strange man? With the help of Budd Hopkins, she was able to trace the man to Cincinnati, Ohio. He appeared to be a normal earthling, except for, according to a friend, he expressed a strong interest in "occult or paranormal phenomena, including UFOs." He also "had a habit of taking off, sometimes for long periods of time, like years, and no one would know where he was or if he was even alive. Eventually he would return as if he had never been gone, with no mention of where he had been all that time."

And that's where the story rests for now. Currently, says Debbie, the man is on one of his long trips and cannot be located.

If aliens at a bookstore, a New York Deli, a campground, a gas-station and a bus aren't strange enough, how about an alien at school?

In the Spring of 1968, Shane Kurz had a series of terrifying close-up encounters with a UFO outside her home in upstate New York. One of those involved missing time in conjunction with physical evidence. Her encounters continued, and she eventually sought out a therapist and went under hypnotic regression. Kurz was then able to recall the period of missing time. To her shock, she discovered she was a UFO abductee and had interacted with extraterrestrials with grayish skin, no hair and large eyes, but otherwise human-looking.

Kurz later recalled a very peculiar incident that occurred approximately one year before her first abduction in 1968. At the time she was in High School. "One days," says Kurz, "I decided to go [to school] early and when I was about fifty yards from the school entrance somebody came up behind me. It was raining and I was carrying an umbrella, and I had not seen anyone on the street prior to that. But suddenly somebody appeared behind me and said, 'Hello, Shane, may I share your umbrella?'

"I turned around," says Kurz, "and saw a man walk up to me. He struck me as being different by the fact that his appearance just didn't seem to fit in with the way everyone looked around my area. His dress was a little more modern, maybe a year or two ahead of ours, so I thought he was a stranger. He had on corduroy pants, and a plaid shirt, but his eyes and ears were the strangest things. I was fascinated by his ears because they seemed to come to a point and were very sharp compared to eyes. Also his eyes were gray, and yet when I looked at them, they seemed to go--as if I could see completely through them. They were very magnetic. He seemed to talk with some kind of accent, but I couldn't quite place it. It sounded a little on the Oriental side. His eyes were slightly slanted, not up but sort of back. His hair was light brown, and he did not wear a hat which was unusual, because it was cold and raining...and he wore no coat either...He wore no necktie, his shirt was open, and he was about five foot four and came level with my shoulder. When he walked, he never took his hands out of his pockets."

Kurz immediately asked the stranger how he knew her name, but he evaded the question and began asking some of his own, all of which were somewhat strange.

He asked Kurz what she did during lunch hour at school. When she told him that she played volleyball or basketball, he asked her, "What is volleyball and basketball?" Kurz told him that everybody knows about these games, but the stranger insisted that she explain the games to him.

Then he asked her, "During your lunch hour, would you like to go for a ride?"

When she replied that she didn't see any car, he pointed to a nearby field and said, "Oh, in my vehicle over there...it is a white vehicle."

Kurz politely declined. Then came the strange part of the encounter. Says Kurz, "I sort of ended the conversation by saying, 'It was nice meeting you,' and I turned around and I think I took three steps-- he didn't follow me--I turned just out of curiosity to see where he went, and he wasn't there. No more than three seconds had passed from the time I took the steps and turned around, and there was no possible way that he could have gotten out of my sight that quickly. I was stunned."

Kurz quickly searched the whole area, but the strange boy had literally disappeared. She asked some of the girls in the area if they had seen the stranger, and they replied, "Who was that cute boy you were walking with?"

This wasn't Kurz's only public encounter. About one month later, she had a similar experience, this time in a convenience store. "I was in the store looking at a magazine," she says, "when a man with very thin, blond hair, hardly any hair on his head, and extremely white skin, kept looking at me. He wore a black overcoat which covered him completely; it seemed almost too long and big for him. I thought perhaps he was an albino because his eyes were so clear-looking. He kept smiling at me and I became somewhat nervous because of his staring and hanging around; he wasn't buying anything, and as I walked around the store getting things, he seemed to hang in back. And when I stopped at the magazine counter and was looking through them, he just kept looking at me in a sort of shy way. He never said a word or anything, but I felt his presence behind me all along. I tried to ignore him. Then I turned around and he was gone."

Again Kurz dashed around looking for the strange man, but he was nowhere to be found. Less than a year later, she experienced her abduction inside a UFO. Inside was the same man she had seen at the convenience store.

Another gas station-alien encounter occurred on March 20, 1988 in LaCross, Wisconsin. On that evening, Professor of Indian Studies and award-winning social activist, Jonathan Hunter Gray and his son, John, experienced a missing time UFO encounter while driving outside of Richland Center, Wisconsin. The encounter was typical in most respects, however, Gray and his son say that they were in no way traumatized. In fact, both spontaneously remembered the full details of the event, and both experienced a number of improvements in their health.

Important here, however, is a very strange event which occurred just prior to the abduction. Says Gray, "An odd thing occurred at a Mobil station at LaCrosse. Just as we were climbing into the pickup after gassing up, a strange-looking little man bundled in a coat and with a 'Greek fisherman's' cap, rushed in a stumbling fashion, from the station to his Volvo."

Gray noticed certain details, including the fact that the man was "very strange-looking" not only because he was so little, but because he was wrapped up in clothes that covered his entire body, even though it was warm daylight outside. The hat was very large-rimmed and hid the man's face. The eyes were covered with sunglasses. At one point, they locked eyes and Gray says that he could distinctly feel the piercing gaze of the strange little man.

Eventually the man walked in a bizarre stumbling fashion into his car, and followed Gray and his some for some distance. "We left the station on a little intra-LaCrosse freeway," says Gray. "He followed us; I slowed down substantially, but he declined to pass. He remained behind us until we took the 14/16 turnoff. In the aftermath of the encounter, our minds were drawn repeatedly to this seemingly insignificant episode."

Another fascinating example of an alien encounter in a highly public place comes from professional violinist and highly respected UFO researcher/writer Timothy Good. In 1961, Good became interested in the subject of UFOs. He began to read and research about the phenomenon. He soon learned that telepathy often plays a powerful role during human-ET encounters, and that many people claim to have made contact with human-looking ETs through this process.

One evening in 1967, Good was staying at the Park Sheraton Hotel in Manhattan. On a whim, he decided to conduct an experiment. For about an hour, he stood in the lobby sending out the mental message, "If there any space people around, let your presence be known."

Good was amazed when suddenly his request appeared to be fulfilled. Says Good, "Finally, as I was about to give up, a very healthy-looking man, about 5'10", came over, sat down beside me and took out a copy of *The New York Times* from his attaché case."

Stunned, Good mentally requested, "If you're a spaceman, touch your finger to your nose."

The response was immediate and positive. Says Good, "Without once looking directly at me, he did exactly as I had requested in my silent message!"

Good was so amazed that he was unable to react as the man quickly stood up and walked away. To this day, he is convinced that he made contact with a human-looking ET right there in the heart of New York City.

New York seems to have a large number of these reports. In the summer of 1969, a young lady was returning home from work on the subway when she had an incredible alien encounter in an unlikely location. Says the understandably anonymous witness, "In the middle of the Seventh Avenue subway rush hour crowd I saw a little man about four feet tall. He had a huge head, but it was the quality of his skin that first caught my attention. It didn't look like human skin, but more like plastic or rubber. I knew he wasn't human. I tried to follow him with my eyes, but he quickly got lost in the crowd. No one else seemed to notice. This disturbed me: I thought I was seeing things."

In one unusual case, a woman not only saw an ET in public; she was abducted. Brenda X., a successful commercial artist and a resident of Bronx, New York, is one of many New Yorkers who have gone public with her experiences. Like many abductees, she believes she has been having experiences her whole life. It started out with flashbacks and partial memories of encounters. Then in 1975, at age twenty, Brenda says she was taken by gray-type ETs from the rooftop of her Bronx home to a secret underground alien base somewhere in the southwest. There she saw several different types of ETs (Nordics, Grays and Hybrids) all working together.

In another abduction, Brenda recalled being made to wear weird "glass or plastic" shoes on her feet. Later, when she read that Massachusetts's abductee Betty Andreasson had described the same thing, she burst into tears. The corroboration of such an unusual detail made her finally accept that she was an abductee.

Another major encounter occurred in 1995. This is one of the many New York encounters that occurred in broad daylight in full public view.

Brenda was eating along at an outdoor café near Battery Park City when she saw the short, hazy silhouette of a gray being approach her table. As soon as it reached the table, the gray being became fully visible and commanded Brenda to come with him. Brenda suddenly found herself holding onto the being as they flew up over the Hudson River and into a dark UFO hovering high in the sky. Inside Brenda was subjected to typical ET examination procedures before being returned.

By now it should be clear that ETs can (and do) appear just about anywhere. Certainly there are a lot of strange characters in any city, especially New York City. However, in this next case, the witness is certain that the character she saw in the middle of the day in downtown Manhattan was "definitely not human."

It was October 1, 1999 in the afternoon. As the anonymous witness writes, "I was ascending the escalator at Penn Station, when I reached the street level, about twenty feet away [I saw] what seemed like a male figure, standing about six feet seven inches, near the mouth of entranceway to the station. Crowds of commuters flowed around him, as though he wasn't there. He stared at the variety of passersby, as though he were trying to choose one of them. I caught a glimpse of his face, maybe his eyes too. I don't remember if he looked at me or not."

The witness looked at the figure for only a few seconds, and then kept walking, too afraid to turn around. Says the witness, "The fear instilled in me was so tremendous [that] to this day I can't explain it. His face was not human. His eyes looked

119

right through you. It was something I wanted to forget as soon as possible, but I couldn't. It was as though he had some kind of will that said, 'Keep walking, don't stop, don't look, this does not concern you.' His face was a light gray, almost white, thick brown, menacing eyes--and the thing that stays in mind the most was his stature, or the way he was standing: his back arched, broad shoulders, his elbows pointed towards his back, his head tilted down just a bit looking at the tops of people's heads, scoping them out."

Besides New York City, another location that seems to have a large number of public encounters is Las Vegas. According to a well-known Las Vegas researcher, in the mid-1980s (exact date unknown), she was contacted by a gentleman who worked in Las Vegas at a major casino. He declined to name the actual casino, but told the researcher that it was his job to sit in a separate room where he monitored the security cameras that had been placed in strategic locations throughout the casino. Whenever he observed suspicious behavior or cheating, he was immediately to report the incident to his supervisor so that action could be taken against the violator.

One day, while monitoring the dozens of video screens, one of them showed something incredible. This particular camera was hidden in the ceiling of the casino and looked down on the table from about a 45-degree angle above.

The video showed that there was a group of six or seven normal-looking people playing cards around one of the tables. However, among this group of people were two strange-looking people.

They were about five feet tall, with slightly larger than normal bald heads and dark eyes and a very small nose and mouth. They were wearing strange white tunics or robes. They appeared to be observing the game as it was being played.

The security officer could hardly believe what he was seeing. Although the figures were humanoid, they were clearly not human. Even stranger, however, was that nobody in the casino seemed to notice them. Often there were some wild characters who came into casinos dressed in strange costumes, but they always attracted attention. These figures were attracting no attention at all, and yet, if they were in costumes, it was the best the security officer had ever seen.

By this time, all the personnel in the video room were gathered around the video monitor watching the strange event unfold. Then something happened which convinced all of them that the figures were *not* human.

The cameras in the casino are hidden very well behind mirrors and other innocent-looking objects. Only a few of the casino employees knew where the security cameras were located. As the security officers watched the video, to their amazement, one of the weird-looking figures lifted his head and stared directly into the security video camera. He clearly knew he was being filmed.

The casino employee who revealed this incident declined to provide further info. The event was quickly covered up, he said, but he did manage to sneak out at least two snapshots taken from the security video, which he provided to the Las Vegas researcher. The photographs clearly show the two figures standing next to the gambling table. The photographs, if true, are nothing less than incredible.

In 1990, David Patterson (pseudonym) was traveling from New Mexico to his home in California when he decided to stop off in Las Vegas for a night of gambling. He went to the Tropicana Casino and played black-jack long into the night. It was the last place he expected to see an extraterrestrial. Writes the witness, "I went to the restroom around 4:00 AM, and on my way back to the tables I stopped and watched a peculiar individual walking up the stairs. This person had a hat and sunglasses on, yet something wasn't right with the way he was walking or climbing the stairs. It looked like he was stuck in mud; his knees sort of came out to the side as he tried raising his feet to take the next step. I noticed also that there were about three more that looked just like him at the top of the stairs, yet some taller. They were all skinny, tall, and I recall noticing their whitish-like hair that seemed to shimmer as if light was bouncing off it. I had never seen hair like this before. My reaction was, what a freak."

The witness reports that at that exact moment, the figure that was walking up the stairs, stopped, turned around and looked at him, as if reading his thoughts.

The witness quickly returned to his table. It wasn't until fifteen years later when he read about the contacts of Charles Hall with "tall whites" in the Nevada desert that he wondered if perhaps he had seen extraterrestrials. The witness was impressed enough that he reported his encounter to NUFORC and several UFO researchers including Linda Moulton Howe and Dr. Richard Boylan.

A truly incredible case of aliens among us comes from David Harris, a drummer who works in the security field in Toronto, Canada. The incident occurred when Harris was a child. The date was May 24, 1958. It was late afternoon when Harris suddenly felt compelled to go to the outside porch of the family home.

Harris's mother and younger brother were already there, and all of them watched when suddenly "a bright white light appeared high in the sky...the light was really powerful, and it got larger and larger as it started to come down toward the 'witch's orchard.'"

The "witch's orchard" was a large grove of Maple trees near the family home. While Harris's brother was too young to observe, Harris and his mother both watched the object land in the fields near their home. "It looked like a craft and it had a bright light like a searchlight...The one thing that surprised both me and my Mom was the way it eventually came to rest in the orchard. There was no crash. The craft landed neatly into position in the field."

The Harris family watched in awe as the craft's lights turned off and two figures, a man and a woman, walked out of the orchard. Harris's mother said, "Those people are from that thing. We are going to follow them and find out where they're going."

The three followed the couple into town, into the local convenience store. Harris's mother sent David into the store to buy popsicles and observe the strange couple. Says Harris, "I could see the back of the man. He had on a pair of long black boots. He wore a black belt. He had a tanned complexion and sandy blond hair."

David entered the store. He reports that he could physically feel the presence of the strange man. "I felt good inside...I felt good as soon as I was standing beside him."

Harris carefully observed the couple. "What stood out in my mind was the gray color of the uniforms the lady and the man were wearing...the lady's long black boots, her thin body structure, her black hair."

As is typical in such cases, the ETs started to ask bizarre questions. "Next the lady looked at me and started asking questions about where they were. She said they were 'time-travelers' or something like that. I felt full of love and power...she then turned to the store-owner and asked him about the cigarettes on the shelf behind him. She kept on asking questions about everything. So I knew that they were not from here. Their dress was really different. Her suit was sort of transparent, but not tight-fitting. She wore earrings. Like the man, she had on a big black belt. I remember that his belt had keys on it, a number of silver skeleton keys fastened to the left side of the belt."

The lady then walked up to David and asked his name. She then spoke to him about religion and Jesus Christ, and told him that he will understand at

124

a later age. "She knew that I saw the two of them come off the ship. She asked me if I would like to go with the two of them into the ship. I said yes, but then her companion interrupted her. She turned to him and he began to talk to her in a different language. It sounded weird, but I felt that I would be willing to go anywhere with them. I felt great trust coming from both of them, love, the greater knowledge of freedom that they had."

After a few more bizarre questions, the strange couple left. Harris, his mother and younger brother followed the couple down the street. Their next memory is waking up in the living room. "Both my Mom and I had been put to sleep and were back waking up at the same time. Mom was sitting at the end of the couch, beside a window...Steve was sitting on the floor. I was out of it. I felt high. I looked at my mom. Her hair was messed up and she was nodding. We were going in and out of consciousness. The first thing she did was look out the window to her right. Then she looked around the apartment and said, 'Oh, look, the popsicles have melted!'"

Researcher David Jacobs Ph.D. has run across several cases of this type. One of his clients, a lady by the name of "Donna," has had visits with an alien hybrid in full public view. "Donna's experiences began when she was a young child," explains Jacobs, "and by the time she was 20, she was meeting with her hybrid in public. One such encounter took place in the summer of 1969, while Donna and some of her friends were on a jetty enjoying the ocean in Maine." When Donna separated from her friends, the hybrid suddenly turned up. He was wearing blue jeans, a jacket and a t-shirt. His hair came down past his ears. He and Donna hid underneath the jetty and he told her he had seen her in a summer stock play the previous evening.

According to Donna, the hybrid told her that he had actually been in the audience watching her perform. Donna had a familiar reaction to her presence. As she says, "He's there and that's all I care about. I can't get enough of him. It's like every pore in my body wants to open up and take him." Eventually Donna was seduced by the hybrid and they had sex.

Afterwards, the hybrid disappeared as mysteriously as he had arrived. Years later, however, Donna says that he visited her again, this time while she was recovering in the hospital after an apparent miscarriage. She also reports other visits from the same person that sometimes ended up with having sex.

Although these cases are still rare, more investigators are coming across them. The first time I heard of one of these cases in person was at a Los Angeles, California UFO Convention. I was sitting at a presentation table signing books and conversing with attendees. I am continually amazed at how many people have profound UFO experiences. On that particular day, a tall pleasant-looking brunette lady approached my table and like so many others, she recognized an opportunity to unburden herself of her UFO experience.

She then proceeded to tell me one of the most unbelievable UFO accounts I have ever heard. At the time, I hadn't heard much about aliens infiltrating society. As best as I can remember, the lady said she was attending a UFO conference for the first time. She had never had a UFO experience, but found the subject fascinating. At some point during the convention, she decided to sit down on a chair situated in one of the hallways and take a short rest.

Suddenly she was startled by a flash of bright light which appeared next to her in the hallway. The light seemed to form smoke or fog, which dissipated very quickly. Out of the fog stepped a normal-looking man dressed in tight-fitting clothes. The man stepped forward and apologized for startling her. He told her that he was actually an extraterrestrial who was visiting Earth on a regular basis. He told her that he had a family on Earth and a job, but that he was often off-planet doing other things, which he neglected to describe.

I asked the lady if she was sure she hadn't fallen asleep, or that maybe somebody was playing a trick on her. And she insisted that no, she had actually seen the strange appear out of thin air. She also wondered if I had heard of any similar accounts. I then asked her for more details, and she described all that she could remember. She seemed sincere and totally perplexed by the experience. She says the man was kind and polite, and that he eventually simply said good-bye and walked away. To this day, she wonders if she met an extraterrestrial.

Abductees were not the first people to report that aliens walk among us. In fact there are some older reports. Many of the UFO contactees, including Howard Menger, George Adamski, Billy Meier, Frank Stranges, Ludwig Pallman and others have made similar claims. Each says that they have not only met human-like aliens, but that these very aliens have infiltrated human society, sometimes to the highest levels of government.

Howard Menger reports seeing a female human-looking ET walking down a public street, and on another occasion, he was medically treated by an ET masquerading as a nurse in an army tent hospital

George Adamski says that he met human-like extraterrestrials first in a hotel lobby, and later in a public restaurant.

Contactee Billy Meier says that the Pleiadian extraterrestrial, Semjase, and her associates often walked among humans, usually for the purpose of obtained certain necessities.

Frank Stranges claims to have met a human-looking extraterrestrial named Valiant Thor, who met with government officials in Washington DC.

Ludwig Pallman, a businessman claims to have befriended a human-like extraterrestrial by the name of Satu Ra, while traveling on a train through India. He later had a visit while in a hospital in Peru.

Ingo Swann claims to have seen a female human-looking extraterrestrial in a grocery story.

These are just a few of the many reports of this particular type. Although some of these contactee cases are controversial, the reports are no more incredible than those of abductees and often come with more supporting witnesses and evidence than the abductee reports. In either case, the point is the same--we may be entertaining not only angels unaware, but extraterrestrials.

Are aliens really infiltrating human society and walking among us? They above account are incredible, however, they are also remarkable consistent. The aliens described are usually either short and bundled up in disguising clothes, or they are described as being exceptionally beautiful or exotic.

David Jacobs believes that these types of encounters will soon increase. "Independent hybrid activity," he says, "is a logical outcome of the abduction phenomenon and the Breeding Program, and it has profound implications for the future of human-alien interaction. It involves hybrids who can, for short periods of time, 'pass' unnoticed in human society, acting independently and free from the presence and control of the grays...Reports suggest that they can exist in human society for about twelve hours."

Jacobs believes that reports of military involvement with abductions is more likely aliens infiltrating society and masquerading as military. As he says, "Late-stage hybrids strive to 'pass' for human, but within limits...In public, they dress like humans, blend into the general population and go unnoticed. They usually wear average casual clothes. The males wear jeans or khakis, t-shirts or long-sleeve shirts...Late-stage hybrids may dress in military-like clothes, such as one-piece jumpsuits that resemble flight suits. Because they look so human, it is easy to mistake them for American military personnel, and many abductees have linked military personnel to their abductions."

Jacobs believes that aliens fully intend to infiltrate society. He calls it step four of the "alien agenda." As he says, "The integration Program: The aliens prepare the abductees for future events. Eventually the hybrids or the aliens themselves integrate into human society and assume control."

Jacobs is not kidding. "I have come to the conclusion," he says, "that human civilization may be in for a rapid and perhaps disastrous change not of our design and I am all the more uncomfortable because the reason for this change is the least acceptable to society--alien integration...with the use of superior technology, both physical and biological, they are engaging in the systematic and clandestine physiological exploitation, and perhaps alteration, of human beings for the purposes of passing on their genetic capabilities to progeny who will integrate into human society, and without doubt, control it."

Obviously Jacobs' opinions are not universal. There has always been a fear that UFOs are here to take us over and that the aliens will one day eat us for breakfast. It is the same force that drives people do demonify the aliens as it is to deify them and call them angels or space-brothers who are here to save the world. Likely the true answer lies somewhere in-between.

Nevertheless, as can be seen, there are accounts on record where extraterrestrials appear to walk among us. And if these few reports are true, there's no telling just how many ETs there may already be walking among us. After all, if they look like humans, how would anybody ever know? They could number in the thousands, or the millions.

Although these cases may seem incredible, they are, as Jacobs says, a logical extension of the UFO phenomenon. So next time you meet somebody who seems just a little bit unusual, remember, you may be entertaining extraterrestrials!

BEHIND THE SCENES: This article was originally published in "UFO Files" (Vol. 1, #8, 1998.) I wrote it after hearing about one of these types of cases firsthand. I was skeptical at first, but as the accounts multiplied, they became hard to ignore. I decided to write an article to see if there were any similarities.

The patterns of the above cases show that aliens frequent public places such as bookstores, gas-stations, stores, schools, beaches, conventions, restaurants, hotels, hospitals, train-stations, on the streets...virtually any public place. They are usually described as having an unusual appearance, including large piercing eyes, pale skin, very short or tall, extraordinarily handsome or beautiful. The dress varies and includes being overly-clothed as if to disguise, odd-looking jumpsuit-type uniforms, or, non-current clothing. Aliens in public places may also behave differently than normal people, often asking bizarre questions, following or staring at people, or responding to telepathic commands.

The most obvious conclusion from these types of cases is something that all UFO researchers eventually learn: UFO encounters can happen anywhere. Since this article was published, several more cases have surfaced, which I have added. If trends continue as they are, there will be more cases forthcoming.

Chapter Seven
The Alien-Clown Connection

Something truly bizarre is happening in the UFO field--something so strange and disturbing that it is causing abductees and investigators alike to take a new look at the UFO phenomenon.

It is well-known that for most abductees, encounters start in early childhood. It is also a fact that an unusually high portion of abductees suffer from a very unusual and unique phobia--fear of clowns. Known as "coulrophobia" it seems to be particularly common among UFO abductees. Is there a connection between UFO encounters and the fear of clowns? And if there is, what is it?

One abductee whose case was investigated by leading UFO abduction researcher Budd Hopkins says, "I have my little idiosyncrasies...as a matter of fact, the only thing that used to scare me as a child--that I didn't like--is clowns. I think I didn't like anything staring at me. And I just don't like clown faces. Julia has clowns all over and I don't like them. I just never liked them."

Hopkins has investigated several cases involving this oddity, including the above case. He writes, "I have encountered at least five abductees with this same dread fear of clowns, in every case dating from childhood. Most cite clowns' scary exaggerated eyes and mask-like painted faces."

But why this fear of clowns? "It would seem that for some abductees," says Hopkins, "seeing the natural human physical body and/or face stylized or distorted triggers memories of the aliens' non-human appearance."

Researcher Raymond Fowler has also run across a few of these startling cases. Concerning one such case, he writes, "We found that Jean had gone through what seemed like a conditioning process conducted by the alien entities. From time to time, an entity would show itself to her, and then disappear. However, it seemed to be dressed in some sort of costume or mask. Jean later would compare the outfit to that of a clown. It dressed so ridiculously that had Jean reported it, no one would have believed her...Jean believed the one who initially came was the same [grey-type ET] but disguised in a clown-like costume and wig."

As the abductee Jean says: "He has a big head! But it's like, like a monster or something...Like something white on him or teeth or some long thing, like funny hair or something...I don't know, like a clown or something."

UFO-clown cases have occurred across the world. After uncovering one of these cases involving a young child who was having UFO experiences, British investigator Peter Hough remarked upon the peculiar role clowns have played in our society. As he says, "The dual motif of the clown--a painted smiling face that is a mask for evil--plays its part in fact as well as fiction, from the Joker in the Batman stories to John Wayne Gacy, the murderer of 33 boys and young men, who worked as Pogo the Clown at children's parties. The clown is the happy smiling face in the car that tries to entice children to take a ride by offering sweets. It has been used to great effect in horror films and books. Yet it also surfaces in the twilight zone that weaves through the UFO encounter phenomenon."

Hough cites one case that illustrates his comments. It all began in the early 1960s when two young English girls, Stephanie and Janice, were playing in a row of abandoned terraced houses that were awaiting demolition. The buildings were old and dilapidated and empty of anything of value.

Says Hough, "One day there were playing in the gutted buildings when Stephanie and her friend Janice glanced through the broken living room window of the house second from the end. Something in the room made them gasp. They called over the other children, but they were unable to see what had attracted the girls' attention. Stephanie and Janice could not understand why. Hanging in an alcove, plain as day, they could see a baggy clown costume. They decided to investigate.

"Inside the walls were peeling and debris littered the floor. There was a strong smell of damp plaster and in places the floorboards had rotted. The girls paused in the doorway of the front room.

"The room was black with mildew, and yet in the midst of all the decay, the costume hung like a sparkling jewel, a tomato-red satin costume with white spots and filly cuffs, ankle and collar. Suspended by a loop was a clown's hat with a white pom-pom sewn on the top. The girls stepped over the threshold into the room."

After looking at the costume, one of the girls finally decided to touch it. Says Stephanie, "All the while I was conscious of Janice standing behind me. I stretched out my hand, and as I did so, the costume shimmered."

The strange effect frightened the girls and they fled. Hough speculates that the costume wasn't really there and that it was some kind of hologram. Later, says Hough, one of the girls became obsessed with collecting "ceramic Pierrot dolls dressed in traditional clown costume."

What do cases like this mean? Was the clown suit being used as bait?

Peter Hough describes another case with equally sinister implications. Abigail began having UFO encounters while still a young child. One night while staying at her grandparents' home, she woke up to find an exceedingly strange figure standing at her bedside. The description of the being is familiar. "It's white with very, very blue eyes. Its face is painted--some sort of clown with a big grin. It's horrible. I hate it."

Abigail claims to have seen this entity dressed like a clown on another occasion, complete with make-up and tights. Again it appears that the entity was using the clown disguise to lure the child into an abduction scenario. Writes Hough, "He [the alien] tried to entice Abigail by telling her she would meet other children, just as Pennywise, the clown entity in Stephen King's novel, "It," used colorful balloons to entice his young victim down the storm drain."

If these case were few in number, it might not be so disconcerting. The truth is, however, that they might be more common than many people believe. In my own investigations I kept running across abductees who experienced a fear of clowns, but had not connected it to any specific alien encounter. While attending a support group of UFO abductees, I mentioned the possible alien-clown connection, and asked if anyone had a particular fear of clowns. Half of them raised their hands and began to spell out just how scared they were of clowns--everything from nightmares to not being able to even watch a movie that had a clown in it.

In at least two cases I investigated, the abductees were not only terrified of clowns, but were able to trace this fear to a specific incident.

The first case involves a lady named Marcellina, a writer and professional chef who had a remarkable alien encounter on February 16, 1994, the day before the Northridge, California earthquake which killed nearly fifty people. The encounter was very complex, involving a long communication with an apparent gray-type extraterrestrial. The case occurred in Topanga Canyon, a well-known UFO hotspot.

As a result of the encounter, Marcellina became mysteriously pregnant. But then, as she says, "about four months later I had a miscarriage and there was nothing in the sac." Although this was traumatizing, Marcellina feels her encounter was ultimately beneficial. Not only did the ET warn her of the upcoming quake, but he also predicted other events in her life, sparked a powerful ability to perform psychic healings, and changed her whole attitude about life.

Another result of the encounter was to trigger a recall of an encounter which occurred when she was just a young girl. She suddenly remembered having seen this ET before.

One night Marcellina was in her parents' living room when she saw a short figure staring at her. "There was this thing standing at my parents' French doors," she explains. "Its face was like a whitish face. The way my mind made it look was into almost a clown-type face. It had black eyes. I was afraid, but I was always confused to know if I was dreaming or not. I basically was convinced I really saw this thing. And it wasn't like a type of thing where it was a person; I know that started when I was young.

"What I remember was, there was a bush with orange flowers. What I did was I made it look like a clown because of the orange flowers near the head. So I always had a fear of clowns since that time. Because it was like someone looking in my window, and why is this person dressed like a clown? But it wasn't really a clown. When I think back now, it was not a clown. But I was always afraid of clowns after that. Like I said, When I really think back on a lot of the stories that happened to me, like that thing I imagine was a clown at my window, I know I was awake. And me making the flowers turn into something that looked like a wig. It was exactly like a cat face without hair, with very big eyes."

Marcellina's experience should sound very familiar. She is admittedly puzzled about the clown-like figure. She is certain she was awake and seeing something, but what? Was her mind interpreting the alien's face to be a clown, or was the alien actually dressed like a clown? It's hard to say, but judging from the other cases, it would seem the latter is possibly true. It appears that aliens sometimes disguise themselves as clowns, particularly when they approach small children.

Another disturbing account comes from Laura Caigoy, a housewife originally from Illinois. Laura has seen UFOs on at least two occasions. One sighting was extremely close-up and involved a number of strange details that indicate a perhaps more extensive encounter than a mere sighting. Furthermore, her young son also has reported seeing strange figures moving into his bedroom and levitating him through the wall with a beam of light.

But before all this, Laura reports an even more bizarre encounter. It occurred when she was five years old, and at the time, it was so strange that she didn't know how to interpret what had happened to her. So she just filed it away for future reference.

As time went on and as Laura realized more and more that UFOs were becoming a part of her life, this one memory kept coming back to her. Finally it got to the point where she could no longer ignore it.

As she related the experience, Laura actually apologized for the bizarreness of the memory. It seemed to her that it was too strange to even have happened. She had no way of knowing that her story matched up closely with the reports of other abductees.

Says Laura, "I was really, really young. I don't remember how old I was exactly, but it was about five. I just remember, it didn't feel like a dream at all.

And I wasn't sick, so I wasn't having one of those fever things. I just remember feeling like there was this person next to me who looked like the joker on a deck of cards. I mean, he was white--a white face-- and had this really big toothy smile. I don't remember what his nose looked like. His eyes were kind of squinty--like on the joker cards.

"He had on a whole outfit. It was velvety, and it was purple and gold. And he was bouncing up and down and making this really weird noise. He looked like he was having a good time. He looked happy. And every time he bounced I would hear this jingling. A harlequin outfit usually has bells on it, but I noticed this one didn't have any bells on it, so I don't know why I was hearing this sound.

"And I looked down and I could see I was naked. I could see the tops of my knees and pubic area. He disappeared around the front of me, and then I felt something. I felt something cold and wet. And then I remember seeing--ah, somebody showing me a knife, like a scalpel. And then a table draped in the same kind of fabric he was wearing. I know this is stupid. I thought it was some kind of abuse thing, but I had no idea what it could have been. I felt as if it was a hidden memory. It was very clear. I can see it all now. I never lost the memory."

Again the pattern is very clear. When aliens approach young children, they disguise themselves as friendly clowns, something that children are usually happy to see.

However, when it comes to adults, the aliens drop the clown disguise and instead take on a huge

140

variety of bizarre disguises, including aliens wearing wigs, cowboy hats and even expensive Armani Suits.

On March 8, 1992, horse-trainer Beth Collings was driving near her farm in central Virginia when she had a very unusual encounter with aliens. At the time, Beth was no stranger to UFO abduction, having had a lifetime of often terrifying encounters. This occasion was no exception.

As she drove along the road her car engine suddenly and mysteriously shut off. She pulled off the road and attempted to figure out what happened to make her car stall. Unfortunately it was nighttime and the road was not busy, so she was unable to even see in the engine compartment. Finally a car did arrive. And so began Beth's bizarre experience.

It was a white sports car which passed her moving very slowly, turned around and passed her again. The driver repeated this maneuver a few times until pulling behind her and parking. Beth watched as a figure approached. "I glanced into the sideview," says Beth, "and saw a tall man wearing a huge Stetson hat walking towards me."

The figure offered to help and began examining the engine with a flashlight. Beth felt unaccountably afraid of the figure and began to notice several strange details. "He wore all white," she says, "and the clothing was very snug-fitting."

Then she heard a telepathic voice ordering her to start the car. As she expected, the engine still wouldn't start. The man told her to go to a house down the street and call for help. Her friend eventually came to pick her up. By that time, however, Beth somehow lost an hour of time.

Having had so many encounters, she knew this was a sign of a possible alien event and therefore underwent hypnosis. Under hypnosis she recalled more bizarre details. As she says, "I could clearly see he was wearing no clothes, yet I couldn't see any navel or body hair and wondered aloud if he was wearing a flesh-colored boy suit of some kind. But that hadn't made any sense, so I accepted that he was probably nude...I first noticed the mustache before realizing he was wearing dark aviator style sunglasses (at night?). I described the head and hat, knowing I had never seen anyone who looked like that, never seen anyone with a head that large...I became frightened though when the man seemed to be telling me something without moving his mouth."

By now Beth was certain that this was no ordinary man. The hat itself was way oversized, spanning an estimated four feet across. Under hypnosis, she realized how large his head was. As she says, "This fellow had a head the size of three basketballs put together inside of a hat that fit him. It wasn't his hat that was big, it was his head that was big...and it looked like he had wraparound glasses on. But the weirdest thing was that he had this mustache hanging down from this little grape of a nose, this thing with a sort of rounded knob at the end."

Beth eventually recalled several other details that confirmed to her that she suffered a missing-time abduction. It was the disguise, however, that really threw her for a loop. As she says, "My logical side, my rational side, tells me something happened to me on that road. And whoever, or whatever it was, thought a real good disguise to relax a horse person would be to show up as a cowboy."

Another remarkably similar case occurred in 1969. Wesley N. Horn describes in his article, "The Alien in the Cowboy Hat" about an encounter in the deserts of southern California with a human-looking extraterrestrial. Horn, a Park Ranger, obtained a description from the witness. Says Horn, "The man told me that the individuals he had encountered looked very much like we do. The most striking difference, he said, was from above their eyes to the top of their head. In exactly what ways, I am not sure, but I believe he said their heads were larger-- possibly indicating a larger brain. For that reason, they told him, they always wore cowboy hats when they visited Earth."

Of course there are other bizarre disguises that seem to be specifically adapted for either the ET or the abductee in mind. One case involved a traditional Chinese woman named Jo Sharp. She, of course, did not see aliens in cowboy hats. The disguise--presumably carefully chosen by the ETs-- was much more appropriate for her personality. She described the aliens which appear in her bedroom as "three feet tall, all of them wearing Chinese coolie hats."

It appears, in some cases, that the aliens' oversized bald heads are particularly frightening to abductees, and because of this, aliens will go to ridiculous lengths to hide this feature. Take the case of a twelve-year-old girl named Glenda, from England. She was in her bedroom one evening when she suddenly noticed she was no longer alone. The case was investigated by English researcher Hilary Evans who writes, "She realized she was not alone in the room, and with her was a strange female who she would later describe as a 'spacewoman' and who, in the drawing made of her, looks like a character from a television science fiction series."

Glenda's drawing shows what appears to be a typical gray-type alien, except for a huge head of curly hair tumbling down the entity's shoulders and back. Interestingly the figure was dressed in colorful, loose shiny clothes--an outfit that looks very much like a clown's.

Other similar cases exist. One lady was in the middle of an onboard UFO experience with tall, slender gray-skinned beings with large round eyes. And like most aliens, they were totally bald. They were speaking to her telepathically, and apparently picked up on her thoughts. As she writes, "I was standing with two of them and noticed that they had no hair...they seemed to be smiling, without moving their mouths. As soon as I thought, 'hair,' one of them seemed to produce reddish gold hair all over its head. This frightened me."

America's most celebrated abductee, Whitley Strieber, reports a very similar onboard UFO encounter of his own. "In this room with me," says Strieber, "were four other beings. The visitor who had come to get me was standing behind me. Sitting behind the desk was what looked to me like a man with a very, very long face, round, black eyes, and a ridiculous excuse for a curly black toupee on his head. He was wearing a green plaid flannel shirt and leaning so far back in his chair that I could see he had on baggy khaki pants and a wide belt. He looked like something from another world wearing the clothes of the forties."

Strieber had another encounter with aliens in disguise. He woke up on the evening of March 15, 1986 to find aliens clustered around his bedside. They stood totally still, just watching him. Strieber attempted to turn on the bedside lamp, but as he says, "I can only describe the sensation I felt when I tried to move as like pushing my arm through electrified tar."

Struggling for any movement, his hand eventually reached the switch only to find that it didn't work. When he looked back to see the aliens, he got the shock of his life. "When I turned my head back," says Strieber, "I confronted a sight so weird I thought afterward that I did not know how to write about it. I still don't, so I am just going to plunge ahead. Beside my bed and perhaps two feet from my face, close enough to see it plainly without my glasses, was a version of the thin ones, the type I have called 'her.' It was not quite right, though. Its eyes were like big black buttons, round rather than slanted. It appeared to be an inept card-board imitation of a blue double-breasted suit, complete with a white triangle of handkerchief sticking out of the pocket. I was overcome at this point by terror so fierce and physical that it seemed more biological than psychological."

The sight so stunned him that he couldn't help but wonder at the purpose. As he says, "The thing before me seemed like a sort of interrogatory.

Why the suit? Did it mean that they were showing me a male?"

Whitley eventually discovered that he was not the only one to see aliens dressed in business suits. As he says, "I found that one of the other people I have met has also had an experience involving visitors in archaic suits. This suggests that the visitors are not too interested in our clothing, or confused about its significance...or perhaps their thought processes have not gotten very far yet in regard to clothing. It may be that, if we ever meet them openly, they will not be quite as naked as the creatures who emerged in Close Encounters. Perhaps they will be wearing double-breasted suits circa 1952, complete with pocket handkerchiefs."

What exactly is going on here? Are the witnesses superimposing an image of clowns and cowboys on the alien's strange-looking faces, trying to make something totally unfamiliar into something they can comprehend?

Or is the clown image something that is projected not from the witnesses, but from the aliens? Perhaps it is akin to the screen memories which abound in UFO encounters. Instead of seeing owls, deer, cats or wolves, many people are also seeing clowns.

Or should these cases be taken at face value? In other words, maybe the aliens are actually dressing up as clowns, complete with make-up and colorful costumes.

It's impossible to say for sure, but after examining all these accounts, the consistency of the descriptions supports the conclusion that the aliens are actually dressing in clown costumes, or Stetson hats, or toupees.

But the real question is why? Why are aliens approaching children dressed as clowns? Why dress as a business man or a cowboy?

As far as clowns, at first glance it might seem to be a somewhat nefarious and deceitful method of enticing and entrapping young children in order to study them or perhaps perform some sort of operation, leaving the hapless youngsters terrified of clowns--something that everybody is supposed to love.

However, there could be a less frightening purpose. There is no doubt that that aliens are disguising themselves, but why clowns? They could have picked any of hundreds of possible disguises, and yet again and again, the clown disguise turns up. Could the aliens be choosing it because as everybody knows--including aliens--most children love clowns?

Could it be that the aliens choose the clown disguise in an attempt to not so much cover their tracks and deceive the children, but to reduce the level of trauma that the encounter might inflict? They may be disguising themselves not so much for their own interests, but for the children's. They could have easily have appeared without any disguise at all. And yet knowing how humans fear anything that looks unusual, perhaps they gave themselves a more benign appearance in the hopes that it would reduce the shock of the encounter.

Hopefully there will be further studies of these types of encounters and the intentions behind the use of alien disguises will be answered. It is simply one more missing piece in the vast puzzle of alien-human relations.

BEHIND THE SCENES: I wrote this article after attending a support group and seeing how prevalent the fear of clowns was. In that meeting, I learned that the clown motif was often used by the aliens. Ironically, if this is being done by the aliens to reduce the fear factor, it seems to have led instead to a widespread fear of clowns, at least among abductees. And the clown motif, I learned, was only the tip of the iceberg. Aliens, it seems, wear a variety of masks.

The article was published in "UFO Files" (Vol 4, No 4, 1998.) Since then, I have heard many different types of screen memories. Witnesses have told me about seeing everything from Teddy Bears to life-sized Barbie Dolls or even Superheroes. It seems that the ETs are doing their best to keep up with popular culture. Often screen memories will appear as animals including wolves, owls, deer, skunks...the list goes on.   Still, many questions remain. Are these disguises for the purpose of reducing fear? Or are they for the purpose of hiding the identity of the extraterrestrials?

After this article was published, the editor called me at home one evening, something he had rarely done. Apparently, he said, a clown (no joke!) had read my article and was deeply offended. The clown wrote a long letter saying that he was going to sue the magazine for defamation. This never happened, but it made me realize that children aren't the only ones being affected by the aliens' use of the clown motif--so are the clowns themselves!

Chapter Eight
The Intimidation & Murder of UFO Witnesses

In July 1947, a spacecraft from another planet crashed in the New Mexico desert. This event marked the beginning of perhaps the greatest cover-up in United States history. Why the cover-up was perpetrated remains a matter of controversy. That a wall of silence was slapped around the case, however, is an absolute certainty.

In the name of National Security, the United States military, or some faction thereof, was given a carte blanc to do whatever was necessary to make sure that nobody knew the truth. In fact, we now know that the military may have gone so far as to murder innocent citizens to guard the secret of the New Mexico UFO crash. Furthermore, the UFO crash at Roswell marked only the beginning of the ruthless policies of our own government in regard to extraterrestrial visitations.

But is this true? Would our own government go so far as to commit murder rather than let the public know the truth? Evidently, yes. There are now several cases on record in which people have been threatened with death or actually murdered because of their involvement in a UFO case.

It all began when the United States military realized that several people had firsthand knowledge or even physical evidence of the UFO crash at Roswell. One by one these witnesses were told in no uncertain terms that if they should reveal the truth about the UFO crash, they would be killed.

One of the first victims of this policy of murder was the Wilcox family of New Mexico. Sheriff Wilcox just happened to be one of the firsthand witnesses to the debris field. Wilcox had told his family what happened.

Then one day, after the debris had been recovered, men in military uniforms showed up at Sheriff Wilcox's office. The military told Wilcox flat out that they would not only kill him, but his entire family.

Even the Sheriff's deputy was threatened. When the deputy was recently contacted by investigators researching the case, the deputy allegedly replied, "I don't want to get shot!" He now denies knowledge of the case.

Another victim was the Rowe family. Frankie Rowe was only twelve years old when her father showed her a piece of metal and told her it was from a crashed UFO. She was, of course, fascinated. However, events then took a darker turn. Less than a week later, the military showed up and asked to speak to Frankie and her mother. They sat the two of them down and basically told them to keep quiet or die. As Frankie Rowe says, "He didn't mince any words...he said they could take us out there in that desert and no one would ever find us again. That was one option. Or they could send Mother and Daddy down to either Orchard Park or Artesia, which was a Japanese prisoner of war camp..."

Literally dozens of people were given this type of treatment. According to leading Roswell investigators Kevin Randle and Donald Schmitt, "Soldiers had also threatened all the firefighters who

152

had been involved. City police officials who had been involved were threatened as well...At Roswell, the government went after everyone who knew anything with threats of prison or death. Agents threatened entire families, expressing a willingness to murder children."

Civilian contractor, Roy Musser was at Roswell base during the retrieval process, and happened to see one of the aliens recovered. Afterwards, Musser was told that "he was never to mention what he had seen to anyone or both he and his family would be in jeopardy."

New Mexico Lieutenant Governor Joseph Montoya was also on the base during the recovery and was present in the autopsy room. Montoya told his friends briefly what he had seen, but then clammed up. As he told his friends, "It's too dangerous. The FBI will do away with you."

Glenn Dennis was the mortician for the small town of Roswell. He had no idea what he was getting involved in when he assisted the military to preserve bodies from a crash. Dennis was at the Roswell base hospital when the bodies arrived and therefore saw more than the military wanted him to see. They quickly moved in with threats. Dennis was told by one military officer that if he talked about the case, he would be "picking his bones out of the sand." Another officer told him simply that "he would make good dog food."

One of the most chilling accounts comes from a nurse who actually assisted in the autopsies of the deceased aliens. She had told Dennis about the bodies and according to Dennis, was in a state of shock. Dennis tried to contact her the next day and was told by base personnel that she wasn't available. The next day he called again and received the same response. On the third day, he called the base and was told that the nurse had been transferred.

Two weeks later Dennis received a cryptic note from the nurse giving an address and telling him that she was unable to communicate with him at that point. Dennis sent her a letter and to his shock, the letter came back marked: DECEASED. Further inquiries regarding her whereabouts revealed that she and five other nurses had just been killed in a plane crash.

Evidently the military is more than willing to carry out its threats against the innocent witnesses. Roswell, however, is not the only case involving death-threats and mysterious fatalities. Roswell is only the beginning of a long trail of blood and dishonor. It seems that whenever a case of high caliber comes along--one involving the presence of physical evidence--the unfortunate witnesses find themselves in a very delicate situation.

Another famous landmark case is the mysterious Maury Island affair. In July of 1947, around the same time of the Roswell crash, the United States was experiencing a dramatic UFO flap. Starting with Kenneth Arnold's sighting of metallic disks over Mount Rainier, Washington, dozens of other reputable witnesses reported seeing UFOs across the nation.

One of these incidents was a sighting over Maury Island in Puget Sound, Washington. Harbor patrolman, Harold Dahl, his son, and a few other witnesses were on a boat in the harbor when they saw six metallic, donut-shaped objects hovering above them. Dahl grabbed his movie camera and began filming. One of the objects appeared to be in trouble and suddenly ejected a huge amount of metallic material into the harbor. Some of the material landed on the boat, injuring Dahl's son and killing their dog.

Dahl immediately reported the event to his supervisor, Fred L. Crisman. The rock-like metal fragments were then collected by the witnesses.

At this point the story takes an interesting turn. Kenneth Arnold, who had sighted UFOs over Washington weeks earlier, heard about the case and went to investigate. Arnold became quickly embroiled in a UFO investigator's nightmare. First came the anonymous threats. Then Arnold discovered he was under government surveillance. Finally a newspaper reporter began to create a very uncomfortable situation.

Arnold, however, continued to interview the witnesses and investigate the case. Dahl then told Arnold that somebody had threatened to kill him if he talked about the case. Arnold learned that the man told Dahl that "he and his entire family would be in great jeopardy should he discuss the matter with anyone."

Dahl then said, "Mr. Arnold, I still think it would be good advice to you. This flying saucer business is the most complicated thing you ever got mixed up in."

Arnold then decided to contact Federal Intelligence Agents from the Fourth Air Force Base

155

at Hamilton Field. Two agents were sent over, Captain Davidson and Lieutenant Brown. The two agents interviewed the witnesses, gathered some of the debris, and said that they must fly back to the base immediately.

Then came the bombshell. The B-25 that was carrying Captain Davidson and Lieutenant Brown and two others crashed, killing only Brown and Davidson. The other two were able to bail-out and parachute to safety.

Three days later, Arnold's co-investigator contacted Major Sander, who was stationed at McChord Field. Sander quickly collected all the material and told the witnesses and the investigators not to talk about the incident. What happened to the debris remains unknown.

The entire truth about the Maury Island incident is shrouded in mystery. That two people lost their lives as a result of the sensitive nature of the evidence, however, remains a strong possibility. That people's lives were threatened is a certainty.

The whole affair ended on a strange note when Kenneth Arnold decided to leave the area. He took his private plane and headed for Boise, Idaho. He stopped in Pendleton, Oregon to refuel and took off again. When he was fifty feet up in the air, his motor went dead. Only because he was a professional pilot was he able to survive. He made a crash landing, breaking his plane in several places. Upon examining the cause of the crash, he was stunned to see that his fuel valve was shut off. The specter of sabotage was raised. As Arnold says,

"...there was only one person who could have shut that fuel valve off--and that was myself."

Another case involving threats and the mysterious deaths of witnesses is the now famous Rendlesham Forest incident in Bentwaters, England. In the last week of 1980, an unexplained light was seen moving into Rendlesham Forest, next to Woodbridge and Bentwaters Air Force Bases, which house a large number of nuclear armaments.

The lights were seen by a number of Air Force personnel, many of whom were dispatched to the scene. The end result was an extremely complicated and extensive encounter involving multiple eyewitnesses of UFOs, metallic craft, and possibly even alien entities. The case generated an uncomfortably large amount of physical evidence. Films and audio recordings were taken by several of the Air Force personnel. Nearby residents and others also witnessed strange lights. Strange holes were found in the soil where the UFO was seen landed in the forest. Numerous animals had been panicked by the incident and many died mysteriously days afterwards. The case involves evidence of virtually all types including radar, photographs, audio recordings, eye-witnesses, landing traces, animal evidence and even a government document from Lieutenant Colonel Halt, admitting that UFOs were seen by base personnel.

What is little known about the case, however, is that the primary investigators were all threatened, and at least two people may have lost their lives as a direct result of their participation in the incident.

The case was first investigated by British UFO researchers Brenda Butler and Dot Street. They had heard about the case from firsthand witnesses and began a preliminary investigation. Discovering that the case was probably genuine, they decided to call up the Base Commander at Bentwaters and ask for an appointment. Surprisingly they were able to obtain an appointment with Squadron Leader, Donald Moreland. On February 18, 1981, they arrived at the base. Moreland had assumed that they were from the Ministry of Defense instead of a local UFO group and was about to kick them out. Then Butler and Street told him that they knew all about the case. Moreland claimed he knew nothing about it, but it was obvious to both Butler and Street and he was lying.

They left the base with little new information. However they were about to have one of the most terrifying experiences of their lives. They had parked their car on the base. As they drove away, their car was functioning normally. They decided to scout around the outskirts of the base and look for the alleged UFO landing site. When they were less than two miles from the actual site, their car was suddenly taken over by a mysterious force. As Jenny Randles says, "Suddenly the car began to accelerate, reaching almost 70 miles an hour. On the rough and bumpy track this was a dangerous speed, creating vibrations which threatened to shake the car apart. As Brenda fought desperately to regain control she had to battle to prevent the car from plunging off the edge into a ditch. Dot, who was beside her, was screaming, believing that her friend was doing it on purpose to scare her...the car raced onwards and Brenda showed Dot that she was not touching the pedals. Whatever was causing it to accelerate was beyond her control. And then suddenly the nightmare was over. The car stalled, bringing the vehicle to a dramatic halt half a mile down the path and deep into the forest."

The two ladies were understandably frightened and sat for a moment in the car. Soon Brenda jumped out and examined the engine. Nothing appeared to be wrong with it. Brenda was not to be deterred and insisted on doing more investigating.

On their way back, the same thing nearly happened again. "Once more the vibrations began," writes Randles, "and the car was forced into a nasty skid although the surface was not wet." Fortunately they recovered control and returned home without any further problems.

Both Butler and Street, however, realized that they could have been killed. They do not know who or what caused their car to malfunction. Although it would be speculation, the explanation which best fits the facts is that Butler and Street were getting too close to the truth, and somebody tried to stop them.

Jenny Randles heard about the case and joined Butler and Street in the investigation, eventually co-authoring the book, "Sky Crash," about the case. Later Randles received more information about the case and wrote another book, "From Out

159

of the Blue." Randles reports that after the first book was published, she received thinly-veiled threats to stop the investigation.

It all began when a well-known scientist called her professing an interest in the case. He promised to call her back after he checked into it. A few days later, he did call her back, but only to recommend that Randles stop investigating the case. The man told Randles, "It looks as if I was on the right track. Something did happen in that forest. You don't know what you've got yourself into...I will not be taking up this matter anymore. I strongly urge that you do the same...You are messing with something for which you can end up at the bottom of the Thames."

Randles was alarmed, but was not about to be put off. She continued her research, and did not receive any more threats. However she did uncover some disturbing details.

At least two witnesses to the Bentwaters UFO landing may have actually been murdered as a direct result of their involvement. Writes Jenny Randles, "Unfortunately, there is a tragic sequel to all this. A couple of years later, when living back in the USA, one civilian witness was murdered. He was attacked and killed for no apparent reason. When I first heard this it was about the time another mysterious death occurred in connection with the case and soon after I had received the phone call warning me about the dangers of investigating the secrets of this episode. Although there is no obvious reason to link the witnesses' death with the sighting, it was nonetheless a chilling reminder."

Another case involving the murder of a UFO witness--a USAF officer--took place at Wright-Patterson AFB, in Ohio. The officer was employed on the base as a computer technician. He had always been skeptical about UFOs, until one day on the job, he discovered a glitch in the computer system, and upon investigation, discovered pages and pages of Top Secret files all about UFOs. The files proved beyond a shadow of doubt that UFOs were real.

Shortly afterwards, however, the man was discovered. Randles investigated the account, and says, "...the man was detained and charged with being in a 1A security area without clearance...the American was arrested, sent off base, stripped of all security classifications and held on a form of 'house arrest.' Four days later, he was involved in a car crash and died. The Air Force investigated the crash and concluded it was a 'tragic accident' and that 'drink' was a factor."

Making someone's death look like an accident may be a method often used to stop any security leaks. This seems to be true in the following case reported by UFO investigator William Steinman.

In 1979, former US Marine Officer Ray Thomas watched the movie Hangar 18 and was stunned to see that the movie portrayed his personal experience while in the military. Believing that the subject of UFOs had finally been declassified, he contacted the Aerial Phenomena Research Organization (APRO) located in Tucson. In July of 1980 he told APRO investigators that he had been involved in a UFO crash/retrieval in June of 1967. He was taken to the site of a UFO crash as a professional guard. He carried full ammunition and also used a guard dog. At first, he had no idea what he and the other guards were keeping such tight security over. But at one point, his dog ran inside the perimeter. He ran after the dog into a tent where a large silver disk was resting on the ground. He was quickly ushered out of the area and warned never to say another word.

Several years later he was discharged from the Marine Corps, but was kept under constant surveillance. Unknown to Thomas, however, he had just opened up a huge security leak. Two days after speaking with APRO, he was visited by two men from an unidentified intelligence agency who reminded Thomas that he was still under a security oath under the National Security Act. He was made to re-sign certain documents and reminded again not to talk about the case.

Two days later, he was visited again by two different agents who outwardly threatened him and told him to get out of the UFO business. Two days after that, a neighbor saw two men trying to break into Thomas's house. The neighbor got a camera and photographed the men.

A few days later, somebody successfully broke into Thomas's house and stole his notes about the UFO crash/retrieval. A few days after that, two government agents showed up at Thomas's home. Thomas pulled a gun on the two agents, called the police and reported that he was holding two burglars hostage. He took the photo IDs of the agents and took photos of them. The police came an arrested both the two agents and Thomas.

The next day, after the police charges were dropped, Thomas returned home. He then made the decision to contact APRO again. APRO referred him to amateur UFO investigator, Ron Curtis. Curtis was employed as a plainclothes police officer in Las Vegas, Nevada.

The two met, and Ray Thomas gave Ron Curtis the photos of the agents' IDs. Curtis turned to the IDs over to his friends at the Department of Public Safety to have them traced. Shortly afterwards, Curtis's boss called him in and was allegedly "very upset" and told Curtis that he had no business in this area.

Curtis attempted to interview Thomas again, but Thomas didn't show up for the interview. When Curtis went to Thomas's apartment, it was empty. So Curtis began an investigation. He tried and failed to get a forwarding address. He began searching for the location of Thomas's new residence. He even called moving companies, looking for information. As a police officer, he was able to run a background check on Ray Thomas and discovered that Thomas held an "Alpha Red Top Secret Clearance." His records checked out, even showing that Thomas was a member of the K-9 Corps attached to the Department of Defense "Special Operations." This investigation was a fatal mistake. Shortly after he started pursuing these leads, he received his first threatening phone call. As UFO investigator Steinman writes, "Ron was contacted by a man who warned him that he was pursuing dangerous lines of research, and he was advised to give it up so that his two orphaned nieces would not be left alone again."

Ron Curtis then got some more bad news. Upon returning to work, he was told that his job in Las Vegas was terminated and he had to transfer to Abilene, Texas if he wanted to keep his job. He asked for copies of the IDs he had turned in, and his boss told him that the information was "highly classified." Curtis had no choice but to move to Abilene. He told his fellow UFO investigators that he had had enough, he was getting out of the UFO business for good.

He loaded up his car and headed with his girlfriend to Abilene. After leaving Las Cruces, New Mexico, Thomas realized that they were being followed by another car. Thirty miles down the road, the car "suddenly moved up fast and deliberately sideswiped the Volks knocking it off the road and into the ditch and Ron was able to keep control by driving down, across and up the other side as always, back down and up the road again." Both passengers felt lucky to have survived and that it was by no means an accident. The car had meant to hit them.

One week later, after they had arrived in Abilene, Thomas's girlfriend was driving the car, when it was again attacked. This time the consequences were deadly. Writes Steinman, "...the little Volks was sideswiped by a big car again, this time knocking it out of control in the beach sand and it flipped, throwing the woman out and landing on her and killing her instantly."

Needless to say, Ron Curtis no longer has any desire to investigate UFOs.

One famous UFO investigator who received threats to his family and himself after investigating

UFOs is newsman Danny Gordon of Wytheville, Virginia. It all began in 1987 when Gordon hosted a live radio show about a UFO sighting that had occurred over Wytheville the previous evening. The show was enormously popular, prompting hundreds of calls. Gordon was plunged headlong into a full-scale UFO investigation. Before long, Gordon himself saw the UFOs and was even able to photograph them. He did another live radio show, which brought even more calls of UFO sightings over Wytheville.

It was shortly after Gordon appeared on the radio program that he began to receive threats. Writes Gordon, "One call I received at home was offering advice: 'Your phone is tapped. You are being watched and followed. You had better stop talking about UFOs.' That was followed by a click and the phone went dead. A letter with no signature told me that the UFO flap involved a secret government operation and warned me to 'leave it alone.'"

On October 23, 1987, Gordon held a live news conference and told everyone that he had photographs of the UFOs that everyone had been seeing. Less than 24 hours later, Gordon's house was ransacked, though nothing of value was taken. Says Gordon, "Between telephone calls of warning, unsigned letters wanting me to halt my UFO stories, and the mysterious break-in, I became a bit paranoid."

It seems that he had good reason to be paranoid. On March 18, 1988, Gordon received another threatening phone call. The caller identified himself as William Lawrence Smith of Clifton Forge, Virginia. He told Gordon a frightening story. "I've

165

been pursuing this thing for many, many years," he said. "I saw my son die of leukemia; he was just as healthy as can be. In fact, I told people I thought they would hit my son to get back at me...the thing is, that anyone who investigates these things usually comes into a whole lot of problems."

Gordon was used to threatening calls, but what Smith said next he found truly alarming. "That's when he got to the part of his call which caught me off guard," says Gordon.

He told Gordon, "If anything should happen to you, if you would come back and some of your friends say that doesn't seem to be the same ole Danny Gordon we knew. He seems like he's different..."

Gordon elaborates: "Smith told me I might come back from Virginia Beach looking sickly, without all my mental faculties. 'What I'm telling you,' Smith said, 'is they will try to hit you if they think it's practical. Most likely it would be done by skin-contact chemicals.' Smith warned that the chemical might be placed on the door handles of my car or on the door of my motel room. Or, Smith added, the chemical might be put on my car's steering wheel. 'The chemical could make you go completely insane or come down with a fatal virus. Uh--they could also come up with something to do your children...if anything does happen to you, you have been forewarned."

Smith told Gordon that the UFOs were flown by humans from a secret society of very powerful people. Smith assured Gordon that he was not a nut, and even urged him to call up the Clifton Forge Chief of Police, who would vouch for Smith. Gordon did just that. As he says, "The next day I called a friend in the Virginia State Police to have Smith checked out. My friend discovered that Smith was indeed known to the Clifton Forge chief of Police."

Gordon considered the warnings carefully, but decided to pursue his investigation. He and co-investigator Paul Dellinger even contacted various branches of the military, all of whom denied any involvement.

Then events took a terrible turn. In July of 1988, Gordon was rushed to the Wythe County Community Hospital in Wytheville, suffering from an apparent heart-attack. Doctors later changed their diagnosis to "trauma of the esophagus, brought on by stress, and from not eating and sleeping right."

Gordon believes that the stress of investigating a UFO wave was the cause of his illness, but one has to wonder if perhaps there wasn't a more sinister cause. That however, would be pure speculation. The intimidation and threats, however, are not. As Gordon said at a live news conference, "I have been advised that my phone has been tapped, and my car bugged, that I was being watched and followed, that I was in danger of being eliminated. It has truly been a very unusual eight months."

After his stress attack, Gordon has slowed down his investigations. He still follows the local sightings, but he learned the hard way that researching UFOs does indeed have its occupational hazards.

UFO witnesses and investigators are not the only people to be threatened by unknown assailants. This treatment of UFO witnesses and investigators has also been extended to many UFO abductees. Leah Haley, Karla Turner and Katharina Wilson are three well-known abductees who have each written a book about their encounters. Each of them reports the same pattern of repeated abductions by both alien and military personnel. In each case, the military threatens the abductees and uses brutal mind-control methods to elicit information about the aliens from the abductees. Other abductees, such as Melinda Leslie and Licea Davidson report the same treatment and say that the military is more brutal than the ETs themselves. One particularly alarming case comes from Karla Turner's book, "Taken."

Angie of Tennessee was first abducted in 1988. This was just the first of what was to be a series of abductions. Angie thought it was bad enough being abducted by aliens, but to her horror, she began to suffer abductions by men in military uniforms. She would be taken to unknown locations where she was questioned about her experiences and threatened to tell everything she knew. Angie learned just how ruthless these people were when she was forced to witness a murder as part of her interrogation. She was surrounded by military men, when a van approached and more men brought out a civilian. As Angie says, "[He] had metal cuffs on his wrists and white tape over his mouth, and appeared to be in a state of panic. Two men carrying black rifles came onto the scene. That grieving man was pushed to the ground, and one of the armed men pumped one bullet into his back."

Angie asked the men why they had killed him. They told her simply, "You talked...We take one like him each time a recruit talks." Angie was told that she would be forced to watch additional murders if she continued to "talk to Karla Turner" about her UFO experiences.

As alarming and unbelievable as these cases may sound, they do follow a surprisingly consistent pattern. Each case that involves threats or murders also has one other common factor--physical evidence. Almost without exception, these people who are threatened or murdered are in possession of (or have seen) some type of evidence would could conclusively prove the reality of UFOs.

These cases also show us how our government deals with people who have acquired physical evidence. They are first ridiculed, then threatened, and if that doesn't work--they are simply killed.

Further proof that this is exactly how the military mind operates comes from files that were allegedly sneaked out of Wright Patterson Air Force Base. The files told the histories of many crash/retrievals, complete with photographs, alien autopsy reports and more.

There was one report, however, that provided guidelines on how to deal with people-- specifically innocent civilians--who knew too much about UFOs. The report was titled: "Elimination of non-military personnel." It listed various ways of dealing with people who had become a problem.

These methods included first disinformation and ridicule. If that didn't work, the witness was to be bribed. If that proved unsuccessful, interrogation and intimidation was suggested, including physical, financial and occupational threats. If that didn't work, they used a method called "psychotronics" to erase people's memories. The final solution was called "termination." This allegedly is done only on rare occasions, and is always made to look like an accident or suicide as it is so risky.

As unpleasant as these accounts are, there are simply too many people saying the same thing for it all to be nonsense. People are being threatened. People are being murdered. The truth is being kept from the public at all costs.

The question is not, is it really happening? The question is, who is doing it and how can we make it stop?

Is it really the United States military that is responsible for all these atrocities? Investigators have proven beyond all doubt that several agencies of our government have a deep interest in UFOs. The Army is well-known to be involved in the Roswell crash. The USAF, CIA, FBI and NSA have all studied UFO as is proven by documents released through the Freedom of Information Act.

But who exactly is killing people in an attempt to perpetuate a cover-up that cannot possibly be contained? It would be a mistake to blame innocent members of our government. It is quite likely that many people in our government have little or no awareness of what is actually happening. Our own U.S. Senators, Representatives,

Governors and Mayors may have little or no idea of what is going on. Even the President of the United States has been rumored to be "out of the loop."

The most popular theory among many UFO researchers is that there an MJ12-like group, composed of civilians, military officials and scientists who attempt to keep a tight control over UFO activity on our planet. This group, assuming it exists, operates on its own rules and answers to no one. Presumably, this group is responsible for the crimes committed against innocent citizens.

These types of cases hold an important lesson. If one should come into possession of incontrovertible proof of UFOs, it might be a good idea to take extra precautions. Secure the evidence. Get photos, extra copies, whatever is necessary to assure that the evidence is protected. The only way to stop these atrocities from occurring is to get the proof out. Once the incontrovertible evidence is released, there will be no need to continue the intimidations, the threats and the murders. And our government of the people, for the people, and by the people will deal with the UFO phenomenon the way it should be dealt with--together.

BEHIND THE SCENES: "The Intimidation and Murder of UFO Witnesses" was inspired by the events that occurred in Roswell in 1947 and the years that followed. The military's record in dealing with UFOs is atrocious. The policy of ridicule, debunking, threatening and going so far as to commit murder is inexcusable. Innocent people have been forced to deal with the trauma of suddenly finding out that UFOs are real, coupled with the additional trauma of being ridiculed, intimidated or worse. Clearly crimes have been committed here, which is one of the problems with the cover-up and the disclosure movement. To admit that UFOs are real would be to open up this can of worms.

Having been a UFO researcher for nearly 30 years, I have had some experience with this. Early on, I began to have numerous phone and email problems. Periodically, when doing interviews, the odd clicks and static would get so bad that even the interviewee would ask me about it.

Back in the days before email, I often had my UFO mail come back opened. This became so predictable that I was able to prove it to family members who witnessed it.

Perhaps the most overt threat occurred when I was had been a researcher for about five years and was just starting to get noticed. While investigating the Topanga Canyon UFO wave, I received a phone call from a gentleman who claimed to be a colonel in the Vietnam War involved in Top Secret satellite mapping. He asked me if I was the Preston Dennett involved in UFO research. I said, yes. He told me, "You know, you're barking up the wrong tree. You shouldn't get involved in something like this. You don't know what you're messing with here. It's dangerous."

Those might not be the exact words, but the message and tone of the call was clear. I replied that I was simply interested in the subject, and the man repeated himself. He changed his tactic and then said that UFO research was a waste of time as "there is no pay-dirt in it." We talked awkwardly only long enough to say goodbye.

I was pretty used to strange calls, but this was a new one. I wasn't afraid, or even angry. Actually I was flattered that the man considered me threat-worthy. I figured it must have been my investigation in the Topanga Canyon UFO wave that caught his attention. I'll likely never know. UFO researchers Jim and Coral Lorenzen, Timothy Good and others have uncovered many cases in which UFO researchers have been monitored by the government. The lesson is clear. If you are a UFO researcher, or if you have any type of UFO evidence--you are being watched!

174

Chapter Nine
Exposed! Project Redlight

When the now famous MJ-12 documents were released, several other documents were also released. One of them was called Project Aquarius, and a paragraph on this document referred to a "Project Snowbird" which stated that "Originally established in 1972, its mission was to test fly a recovered alien aircraft. This project is continuing in Nevada..."

Project Snowbird may be part of another top secret operation called Project Redlight. In the fall of 1989 issue of UFO Universe, Milton William Cooper released some of the results of his research. In the article, "Classified Above Top Secret: Operation Majority," Cooper stated that Project Snowbird was "established as a cover to Project Relight."

About Project Redlight, Cooper said that "...its mission was to test fly recovered alien craft. The project was postponed after every attempt resulted in the destruction of the craft and the death of the pilots...Project Redlight was resumed in 1972. This project has been partially successful. UFO sightings of craft accompanied by black helicopters are Project Redlight assets. This project is ongoing in 'Area 51' in Nevada."

It is interesting that Cooper mentions unmarked helicopters. There is a well-known UFO case known as the Cash-Landrum case. On December 29, 1980, Betty Cash, Vickie Landrum and Colby Landrum encountered a UFO on a lonely

Texas highway. The UFO, however, was surrounded by nearly 20 helicopters of definite earthly origins. Why would a UFO have 20 helicopters escorting it above a highway? Could this be evidence of Project Redlight?

The unfortunate witnesses, especially Betty Cash, suffered what appear to be radiation burns. Betty's eyes swelled shut, she suffered hair and skin loss, nausea, diarrhea, stomach cramps and headaches. She had sores on her hands that persisted even after eight months.

Other people have witnessed UFOs that don't seem to be piloted by beings from other planets. One such case was picked up by Lucius Farish's "UFO Newsclipping Service." Rick Murray told the story in his article: "Is that thing a UFO, or the USAF?" The incident took place in the 1960s in New Jersey. According to Murray, his father saw a typical saucer-shaped UFO while traveling on Route 70. Another witness in a separate car also observed the object. As they were watching it, Air Force personnel drove up in jeeps and tried to convince the men that what they'd seen was their imagination.

The case would be just like many others except for two things. As Murray says, "...the heads my father saw through the portals were human. And along the craft's fuselage, in bold print, were the letters USAF."

Again, it seems, the military is in possession of flying saucers and is flying them around.

Another account was told in the Volume 3, No 4 1988 issue of the California-based magazine, "UFO." Bill Hamilton's article, "The Military's Secret

Space Program," contains the story of someone who claimed to actually work in "Area 51" of the Redlight Project in Nevada. Writes Hamilton, "In the early 1960s, a radio technician working at Area 51 reported seeing a saucer on the ground, some 20 or 30 feet in diameter. He said when it flew through the air, it was silent. The technician also claimed to have viewed a number of wooden shipping crates marked 'Project Relight.' That project may have been a forerunner to something called Project Snowbird."

In July 1975, two boys (ten and fourteen years old) were playing in the graveyard near their home when the older boy said, "What's that? Look!"

The ten-year-old (now an adult) describes what he saw: "I saw a large circular disc coming towards us. It went almost over our heads. It was about 100 feet off the ground and about 25-50 feet in diameter. It was a light gray color and had the letters, 'USAF' on the bottom of it on one side and an alpha numeric on the other side."

"It's a flying saucer," the ten-year-old told his fourteen-year old cousin.

Says the witness, "After it flew by us, it stopped in mid-air, hovered for a few seconds and descended to land on the other side of the wooded area south of the cemetery. It made an electric humming noise with a slow pulse and an air-rushing noise."

The boys approached the landed craft and saw "two dark silhouettes" exit the craft. One of them held a bright red flashlight in his hand. The children ran home and told their aunt who thought they were joking.

Their aunt wouldn't let them outside, though they later visited their grandmother's house and shared the story with their uncle and older cousins. Again, they were not believed.

The children got some vindication when the next morning, there was some very unusual things happening in the graveyard where they saw the USAF-UFO. Says the witness, "In front of the cemetery gate was the town marshal, blocking the entrance, and two Air Force trucks in the cemetery. At the end of the cemetery was an Air Force helicopter. The marshal told us that the helicopter had engine trouble and had to be repaired."

The witnesses insist, however, that what they saw was not a helicopter. "It was a circular disk and had the letters 'USAF' in big, bold, black letters on its bottom. The helicopter was Air Force blue with the letters 'US Air Force' on its side. Obviously not the same craft."

The witness is convinced the UFO he saw was piloted by humans. "I believe it landed and it needed a repair and that the helicopter came from Grissom AFB to fix it and the pilots may have seen us, and that's why they kept the helicopter there as a cover story."

Such stories may seem rare, but they might be more common than most people realize. By pure luck I was able to procure two separate accounts that seem to be evidence of Project Relight, the alleged Air Force study to fly UFOs acquired through crash/retrievals.

The information for the first account was told by a friend of my father's, who knows one of the

178

central witnesses of the case. The information was gained through two or three casual conversations, each talk eliciting more data.

This case involves two people--neither of whom would give their names. I'll call the first person, Greg Edwards, and the second, Tom Matthews.

Greg and Tom were best buddies and considered each other blood brothers. Greg thought he knew everything there was to know about Tom. Then one day, Tom approached Greg with a startling revelation. Tom said that nearly everything he had told Greg about his life wasn't true--that he lied about his job, where he worked, what he did--everything. All lies.

Tom then told Greg what he really did for a living. What Tom revealed about his work is the stuff of science-fiction, but Tom insisted that it was all true.

Tom's story began in high school. He was extremely bright and had received an exceptionally high score on the Scholastic Aptitude Test. In fact his scores were so high, it caused some attention to be paid to him. It seemed that the United States Government was very interested in Tom and wanted him to work for them. He had no idea then what his high scores were going to cost him.

Government officials first approached Tom's parents, and asked them if they would allow their son to work for the government. When Tom's parents gave their consent, Tom was approached and given an offer he couldn't refuse. In exchange for his services, he would receive a Top Secret clearance

179

to match a ridiculously large salary. His job was to conduct research in a Top Secret underground base in Alaska.

Tom accepted the offer and went directly out of high school and into government service. He told everyone he was stationed in Nevada--but this was only a cover story. In reality Tom spent only weekends in Nevada. On weekdays he flew by private military jet to a Top Secret government base in Alaska.

The base was an eight-story building located almost entirely underground. The base financed itself by setting up the world's leading drug smugglers. Officials would arrest the drug smugglers, confiscate all the money and the drugs, then turn around and sell the drugs back to another smuggler--whom they would then proceed to arrest and confiscate. It sounds like a strange way to finance a scientific-military research base, but it's obviously very profitable. Although not strictly legal, such practices were done in the name of National Security.

Tom reported that the base was mainly a research station that nabbed up some of the best scientific minds in the country, and had the latest technology for advanced research. There were three major areas of research of which he was aware.

First, the base researched and developed biological weapons, which, as Tom said, made all other weapons look like child's play.

Secondly, the base researched and developed electronic sensory and detection devices that allowed telescopic sight through solid objects, such as walls.

Thirdly--and most importantly here--the base also researched and developed electromagnetic propulsion devices--flying craft which needed no fuel to operate other than the Earth's magnetic field. According to Tom, the ships looked like UFOs, and are able to hover silently, and move at astonishing speeds. As Tom says in his own words, "Some of the UFOs seen over Alaska are probably ours."

Tom didn't say exactly what his job at the base entailed, but he did say that the security was extremely high. Every week he was subjected to a horrible ritual. Due to the nature of his job, everything about him had to be known. He would be taken to a special room where he was given a dose of Sodium Pentothal and put into a hypnotic trance. For a period of a couple of hours, he would be interrogated into every aspect of his life for the past week. Every detail would be laid bare to make sure that there were no security leaks. This agonizing ritual was repeated every week for as long as he was at the base. There were no exceptions.

Tom finally got out of the business after several years because the lifestyle was too harsh. Since he left the base he has been, and still is, under close monitoring by the government. After his release from the base, he was offered several extremely high-paying jobs by some of the country's leading corporations. Tom declined these officers and pursued a more modest job and lifestyle.

So closes Tom's story, which alone could be easily dismissed. But in addition with those collected by the other researchers, it seems evident that the government is in possession of UFOs, and are in fact, flying them around.

I received further confirmation of this from a man named Jonathan, who was at one time employed by the United States Air Force. Jonathan worked as a Flight Commander Trainee at Anniston Air Force Base in Alabama. One evening in late 1976 while walking the base grounds with his friend, they encountered a metallic disk with yellow lights around the perimeter. Jonathan and his friend both suffered a period of missing time, and were left convinced that UFOs were real. But Jonathan never thought the subject would cross his path again.

Later, after Jonathan left the military, he was told a strange story by a man I'll call "Bill." Bill is the brother-in-law of Jonathan's ex-girlfriend.

Bill was employed by the Central Intelligence Agency. Jonathan noticed that every winter, Bill would disappear for the season. When the cold was over, Bill would reappear with a deep, dark tan and a strange tropical disease that he had contracted from some exotic unknown country.

At the time Jonathan knew Bill, Bill was a retired CIA agent, (if there is such a thing, as Jonathon pointed out) and was currently employed as a private detective. The subject of UFOs came up one day, and Bill told Jonathan what he had found out while working for the CIA.

Bill said that he knew firsthand that the Air Force had in its possession a crashed UFO, and that alien bodies had been collected by the military where they were being studied. Bill told Jonathan that the aliens were pretty much human-like, but that their organs were all messed up--that their heart was located in their rectum, the blood-pressure was way off the scale, along with other strange abnormalities. Bill further states that he knew that one of the aliens was kept alive, though all the others died when the UFO crashed.

But that was just the beginning. Bill then stated that the government was not only holding a number of crashed UFOs, but that they were flying them around. Bill said they would fly above the interstate highways in New Mexico. They would travel late at night, and would go from base to base. This was apparently a regular practice--one which resulted in an inevitable accident.

According to Bill, the UFOs were manned by military personnel. One night a military-owned UFO crashed directly on an interstate highway in New Mexico. Bill said that the entire highway was completely cordoned off around the crash site, and the highway was closed down. Because it was impossible to keep the event entirely secret, the media and public were misinformed that it was simply the crash of a military aircraft. The UFO and all traces of it were quickly recovered.

Jonathan was quite taken aback by Bill's story and said, "This is dangerous information. Why are you telling me this?"

Bill said, "It doesn't matter because nobody will believe you anyway," and made an insinuation that those who knew too much mysteriously disappeared.

Jonathan was shocked by the information. Because of his previous encounter, he was certain that UFOs were real, but he had no idea that UFOs had crashed and been recovered. And he wasn't sure if he was happy knowing about it. He asked me if I had heard of anything like this before and was quite surprised that I had. He kept saying, "Really?!" as I related similar stories to him. It was obvious that he thought UFO crashes were unheard of.

UFO crashes are much more common than many people realize. The subject first came to attention with Frank Scully's book, "Behind the Flying Saucers." Perhaps the most well-known and best-documents case was first revealed in Charles Berlitz's and William Moore's book, "The Roswell Incident."

Soon other books began to reveal more accounts of UFO crashes, such as Raymond Fowler's, "Casebook of a UFO Investigator," and William Steinman's "UFO Crash at Aztec."

The first comprehensive studies into UFO crash-retrievals were done by Ohio-based researcher Leonard Stringfield. He uncovered information about UFO crashes and wrote about it in his book, "Situation Red: the UFO Siege." When reports continued, he privately printed his "Status Reports", which tell dozens of cases of UFO crash-retrievals. Today there are many well-documented cases and many books have been written on the subject. If there is a cover-up of UFO evidence, it definitely has a few leaks.

It should be obvious by now that the United States Government does in fact have in its possession crashed UFOs and alien bodies. The preceding accounts, if true, indicate that not only does the government own a few UFOs, but that they are flying them around. Project Redlight seems to have been a success.

BEHIND THE SCENES: "Project Redlight" was published in the May 1990 issue of the new magazine, UFO Universe, edited by longtime UFO researcher Timothy Green Beckley. I had only written a few UFO articles, and this was the first one I had ever sent to him, so I had no idea what to expect. I was delighted when I received a call from him telling me that he would like to publish the article. It became the first of dozens of articles I would later published in UFO Universe and several other magazines which Beckley also edited. Years later Beckley told me that of all the articles I had ever sent to him, this first article remained one of his favorites. Today there are many accounts of reverse-engineering at places like Area 51 and Wright Patterson AFB and other locations.

186

Chapter Ten
Mining Data on UFOs

One of the greatest mysteries surrounding the UFO phenomenon is: *Why are they here?* Most researchers agree that there are probably many reasons. The most popular theory by far is that UFOs are scientists and tourists, here only to study and observe. However, the ET agenda appears to include a wide variety of goals, including abducting humans for genetic material, imparting warnings about the destruction of our environment, hovering over and studying nuclear power stations and other technological installations, collecting samples of flora and fauna...to name only a few types of UFO activity.

Another reason that has been raised to account for UFOs' interest in planet Earth is *mining.* It may seem hard to believe that with their advanced technology, UFOs would need to travel all the way to Earth only to dig for precious metals. On the other hand, perhaps UFOs require rare metals for their craft.

Whatever the explanation, the number of cases involving UFOs and mines speaks for itself. Some of them provide very convincing evidence of UFO reality. Let's examine these cases and see what they reveal about the UFO occupants and their agenda on Earth.

Belgian-Congo Mines

According to a 1952 CIA document released through the Freedom of Information Act, numerous witnesses observed two "fiery disks" perform incredible maneuvers directly over an active uranium mine located near Elizabethville in the southern part of Belgian-Congo. The objects hovered over the mine for at least fifteen minutes during which they glided in "elegant curves" and "changed their positions many times."

When it became apparent that the mine was the target of the objects, Commander Pierre of the Elizabethville Airfield decided to take off and pursue the objects in his fighter plane.

He chased them for fifteen minutes, during which time they evaded him by dropping down to about 60 feet above the treetops, and finally speeding away at an estimated speed of more than 800 miles per hour. According to the CIA report, Pierre was considered a "dependable" witness. No explanation of the incident was included in the report.

Brush Creek Titanium Mine

In 1953 one of the world's most unusual UFO-mine encounters took place outside a small isolated northern California town called Brush Creek. Today it remains a classic case in the UFO literature. The entire ordeal revolves around two titanium miners, John Black and John Van Allen, who had a series of encounters while working at their mine.

In early 1953, both Black and Van Allen observed a "metallic saucer" hover above the area of the mine. Over the next few weeks, the object returned on four separate occasions. On April 20, their concern mounted when Black saw the craft again from a distance of a quarter mile. It was obvious to the witnesses that the UFO had a strong interest in their mine.

Exactly one month later, at 6:30 PM on May 20, Black was returning to the mine when he saw the now familiar saucer rising up from the sandbar at the junction of Marble and Jordan creeks. The craft quickly took off towards the east and disappeared. On inspecting the area, Black found several small five-inch footprints.

Then exactly one month later again, on June 20, Black approached the junction of the two creeks when he saw what he thought was a small child with a bucket. At that point, he saw the large saucer landed nearby on the sandbar. Black examined the figure which he said appeared to be a small man wearing green pants, unusual shoes, a jacket and a green cap. He was very pale and had black hair. Says Black, "He looked like someone who had never been out in the sun much."

Black watched as the man scooped up water with an unusual cone-shaped bucket. Black had approached to about forty feet when the little man heard him and quickly entered a small metallic saucer that was landed on a sandbar. At that point, the craft took off quickly and in total silence, leaving Black amazed.

Somewhat concerned, Black contacted Brush Creek sheriff, Fred Preston. Black jokingly asked the sheriff if it was "open season on space men." The sheriff, however, remained serious. "I told them they'd better grab it next time so they'll have something to back up their story." Preston then told them he couldn't give them permission to shoot. He did, however, contact the Air Force.

The story was then leaked to the press and so began one of the strangest events in UFO history. Because the saucer had appeared on April 20, May 20 and June 20, everyone was predicting a July 20 landing. More than two hundred people arrived on the scene with cameras waiting. Residents of Brush Creek, newspaper reporters, cameramen and saucer enthusiasts all converged on the scene. Snack bars and chairs were set up as if people were going to watch a circus performance.

Unfortunately it was a total bust. The expected UFO did not arrive and the Brush Creek ordeal came to a sudden close. However the case has never been solved. The miners were well-respected and their testimony was backed up by Vi Belcher, owner of the local store who said they were "not drinking men."

The account was investigated in depth by researchers Gray Barker and Paul Spade, both of whom were actually jailed by the Brush Creek sheriff's station when they tried to conduct a stake-out for the saucer. Both came away convinced of the veracity of the case. Says Barker, "Spade made what I considered an objective investigation and reported that the story was evidently not a hoax...Whatever Black saw, the story sounds almost too good for someone to think up, especially when such a story is credited to an isolated miner who is not likely to be at all well-read on science-fiction."

Paraburdoo Iron Mine

Located in the Pilbara region of Western Australia, (about 950 miles northeast of Perth) Paraburdoo is a small mining town of about 2500 inhabitants. UFO researcher Ellis Taylor had received several reports of UFO sightings from the area in the past. Then one day he received another report. In this case the witnesses were able to take a series of photos as the object hovered directly over the local Paraburdoo mine.

The encounter occurred at 7:10 PM on August 30, 2006. The main witnesses are Rob & Jules, residents of the town. While sitting in their backyard, they and their children observed a "bright light" moving at a leisurely pace above the street at about treetop level. The light was oval-shaped and flashed orange and yellow.

The family watched as the object headed toward Radio Mountain and the Paraburdoo mine. Upon reaching the base of the mountain the object moved sideways, turned bright red and began to ascend up the side. Shortly later it reached the top of the mountain and the location of the mine, where it stopped and hovered.

Realizing that the object was unusual, Rob grabbed his camera and snapped several pictures. Meanwhile Rob's neighbor Dave and his four children also observed the object. After about ten minutes the object began to rise slowly. It was a clear night and the small group of witnesses was able to watch the UFO until it became a small red dot high in the sky and finally disappeared.

Rob's neighbor Dave turned to everyone and said, "I think we've just been visited by aliens."

Unknown to the witnesses, other witnesses in Paraburdoo also observed the object. Researcher Ellis Taylor is convinced not only of the sincerity of the witnesses, but that they saw something genuinely unusual. Says Taylor, "They are a tight-knit community, born from their isolation, where get-togethers over a cold beer or ten and a barbie are everyday occurrences. They are good people, honest and down-to-earth. They don't waste their words and if they say they saw something, they did."

Certainly the witnesses are convinced. Rob and Jules write: "This experience for us was the most awesome thing we have seen in our lives as we do believe we are not alone."

Tucson Gold Mine

There are dozens of cases on record in which UFOs have been seen hovering over various mines. A stunning example occurred on December 28, 2001 over a gold mine in the desert outside of Tucson.

"I am a regular guy," says the witness. "I am a four-year veteran of the Army...I have an Associate's Degree in structural engineering, and an advanced degree in heavy equipment operation. My name is Barry."

Barry was running the night shift, using a track hoe to feed an incinerator. His co-worker was a retired special forces Major. A winter storm was moving and there was a cloud ceiling at about 9500 feet.

Looking up, he was shocked to see an "immense craft" hovering over a nearby mountain, directly above a gold mine. Using the highway to gage the size, Barry estimated that the craft was more than a mile long. It had a row of sequential running lights which illuminated the cloud cover above it.

Says Barry, "My esteemed colleague got a deathly white sheen to his face and would not come out of his personal jeep...he was scared and he was babbling like a child. Me, I turned the track hoe to face it and kept flicking my day-lighters in the hope they could come and see who was behind those lights...I felt at ease--no panic. You see, I felt as these were my friends, like we had met before."

The object disappeared and reappeared two more times in slightly different locations, but "never too far from this gold mine it was hovering over."

The next night, two military attack Cobra helicopters hovered over Barry's jobsite and just sat there in the sky until Barry finally turned on the floodlights. At that point, the helicopters circled the jobsite several times and then took off "directly towards that gold mine."

Two weeks later, Barry's co-worker quit, and made it clear that he never wanted to talk about what happened. Barry, however, says that he has had encounters in the past. Less than a year after the sighting, he reported it to the National UFO Reporting Center.

Pima Copper Mine

Just after midnight on July 22, 1971, an anonymous witness observed a strange "flat disk" with a "teardrop-shaped tail" and a bluish-glowing light around its exterior. The craft moved at a leisurely 45 MPH, directly over the west side of the waste dumps of Pima mine, about thirty miles south of Tucson, Arizona.

The witness was about 100 feet away and watched the craft rock back and forth, clearly under intelligent control, until finally darting off to the north. Only one week earlier, the witness saw another (or the same) craft moving from south to north, then turning at a right angle and moving off to the east where it disappeared.

He speculates that the craft are attracted to the area because of the mine. As he writes, "There are several very high voltage high power lines supplying power to the mine plus a continual thermal updraft from the open pit copper mine."

Another case in the same area occurred in November of 1980. George Parks was driving home late at night after working the night shift at the BHP Copper Mines in San Manuel, Arizona when his life changed forever. "Coming around the bend at Oracle Junction," says Parks, "I saw a metallic craft hovering not far from the road. I saw seven windows. Behind every window stood a figure. An instant later, it flew off."

Parks was amazed by his sighting. He was in the military for more than 20 years and never saw anything like that. He joined MUFON and became a field investigator. Before long he became the Pima

County Section Director for MUFON, and later the Arizona State Director. Says Parks, "I'm still looking for answers."

Lavender Pit Copper Mine

On June 27, 1947, (only a week before the Roswell UFO crash) John A. Petsche, an electrician employed at the Phelps-Dodge copper mines in Bisbee observed a silver mirror-like disk-shaped object move overhead. The object was silent and wobbled slightly as it moved.

Two other men working with Petsche also observed the object. All three agreed the object was unusual.

A mile and a half away three other mine employees including John Rylance (an electrician), I.W. Maxwell and Milton Luna reported watching the object--which they described as oval-shaped--move lower and lower until it suddenly landed on a hill nicknamed Tintown.

The object then took off, leaving a group of stunned miners. Reporters learned of the case and converged on the scene. Vernon C. McMinn, the gang boss for the group of electricians who had observed the object told reporters that several other employees at the mine had also seen the object and described the same thing.

Unknown to the mine employees, Major George B. Wilcox of the US Army observed eight or nine light-colored, disk-shaped craft move at a low elevation over the Bisbee area at the same time of the Bisbee mine sighting. The objects were evenly spaced in single file and moved with a dipping "rocking" motion.

Years later, in the 1980s, the UFOs came back for another visit. On this occasion, the witness (a former rocket scientist who worked as a telemetry collector and analyst for the NSA) was at a gas-station only a few hundred yards distant from the Lavender Pit copper mine, in Bisbee, Arizona. Suddenly he had a strange feeling that something was hovering above. Looking up, he saw a large metallic object about 250 feet up, glint in the setting sun. It appeared to be a metallic oblate spheroid, like a squashed sphere, about 100 feet in diameter. There were no signs of any rivets or seams and looked absolutely perfect. It was rock-solid stationary in the sky. "Do you see that?" he exclaimed to the gas-station owner.

"I sure do!" the gas-station owner replied.

They both stared in awe at the object, which was silent except for a low humming noise. It was so low to the ground that the witness considered throwing a stone at it, but decided that his actions might seem "unfriendly." Both he and the gas-station owner felt that they were being observed by the occupants of the craft.

Several cars drove by, slowing down as they saw the object and then racing away along the road which winded along the circumference of the pit mine. Says the witness, "Nobody stopped, although they could be seen leaning down and forward briefly to get a better look."

After several moments the craft wobbled slightly then moved at a slow pace directly over the mine for about a mile, then suddenly accelerated at extremely high speed upward toward the Queen Mine near Old Bisbee and took off to the west. Shortly later, the witness left the gas-station and was driving toward Old Bisbee when a jet fighter plane appeared, flew over the mine at a few hundred feet and followed the exact pathway of the UFO. Says the witness, "Our government knows about these things. Who is kidding who here?"

Were the ETs looking for copper? Another case (which occurred less than 200 miles away and a few months later) may provide the answer. On October 23, 1980 five men in Morenci, Arizona observed a large dull-black, boomerang-shaped object approach the smokestacks of the local copper smelter plant. To their surprise, the object hovered over the smokestacks, sending down a brilliant beam of light into each one. At one point it dropped a small fireball. After about five minutes, the object moved quickly to the southwest.

One of the men, Joe Nevarez, wished that the object would return so he could see it better. At this point, the men were shocked to watch the object perform an instant reversal. It approached again, this time hovering over the slag dump of the smelter before moving north.

Researcher Richard Haines points out this case as an example of a CE-5, meaning the object's behavior was affected by the witnesses, in this case, by Nevarez's mental command for the object to return. The incident received national publicity.

According to the International Center for UFO Research (ICUR) in Scottsdale, throughout the

1980s, a huge boomerang-shaped object nearly a half-mile wide appeared repeatedly over the small town of Morenci. One sighting in particular was seen by hundreds of the residents. The object hovered in place for long enough so that everyone who was outside was able to see it. More than a hundred members of the Morenci High School observed the object, and described it as being "several football fields" in size. People throughout the town also watched it. The witnesses all agreed that it was covered with red and white lights on the underside which swept back in a boomerang shape.

Brian Myers of ICUR says that the same craft has also been reported frequently over the Hopi and Navajo reservations in the northeastern part of the state.

Gualcamayo Gold Mine

Located in the San Juan Province of Argentina, the Gualcamayo gold mine is an open-pit, heap-leach mine. On December 20, 2008, about twenty mine workers were heading back to their shanty for a break when one of them noticed something odd in the sky hovering over the mine area. He alerted his companions, one of who quickly held up his cell-phone and captured a digital image of the object.

Meanwhile back at the mine, an additional 25 workers observed the object overhead. The moment it appeared, a loud, mysterious buzzing noise swept over the site. All machinery unaccountably failed and drilling operations came to a sudden halt.

Moments later both groups of mine workers watched the object dart away. Immediately all the machinery began to work again.

Local newspapers were contacted, and the story appeared in the *Diario de Cuyo de San Juan*, where it was widely circulated, generating various explanations such as "service balloon" or "a garbage bag flying aloft in search of fame."

Those who observed the object, however, insist that they saw a genuine "ovni" or UFO and point to the strange electromagnetic effects caused by the object, not to mention the photograph.

Pine Bush

Solidifying the UFO-mine connection are events that occurred in the mid-1980s in Pine Bush, upstate New York. Beginning in 1980, researcher Ellen Crystall was searching for a UFO hotspot where she might see UFOs firsthand. When she read a UFO column by Harry Lebelson in *Omni* magazine, she called him up and asked if he knew of any areas of high activity. Lebelson mentioned Pine Bush, and told her about a couple he knew, "Bruce and Wendy" who claimed to be having close-up UFO sightings on a regular basis.

In July of 1980 Crystall and Lebelson drove to Pine Bush to begin a firsthand field investigation. They soon learned that activity in the area had been fairly regular since at least 1969, and had been reported by a wide variety of Pine Bush and nearby Crawford residents, including a policeman, a barber, store clerks, laborers and others (also famed abductee and author of Communion, Whitley

Strieber whose cabin was located in Crawford.) Business owners and downtown employees had allegedly seen UFOs directly over their stores and offices.

Crystall and Lebelson interviewed Bruce and Wendy who had been seeing the craft for several years, including several close-up sightings and landings. They said the craft returned on a nearly *nightly* basis, and that they could see them practically anytime. They promised to show Crystall and Lebelson where the UFOs were appearing.

It was around 10:00 PM on July 18, 1980, as Crystall, Lebelson and her new friends drove east on Hill Avenue and parked next to a certain remote farm pasture. Bruce assured her that the UFOs would soon arrive.

To Crystall's shock the UFOs showed up right on schedule. She and the others observed several strange triangular-shaped craft which moved silently and slowly at about treetop level.

Crystall was amazed and began to trek to the area to see the UFOs again, eventually taking hundreds of pictures of the alleged craft and writing a book, *Silent Invasion,* about her investigations.

At one point Crystall began to wonder why this particular area of upstate New York seemed singled out from other areas to have so much activity. Why were the UFOs continually landing and rising up from these fields? What could they be doing and why here?

She had already interviewed many local residents who told her that they believed the aliens were mining the area. During the summer of 1985

Crystall not only continued to see multitudes of ships hovering in the skies of Pine Bush, she also noticed another strange phenomenon. On numerous occasions she and other witnesses observed what appeared to be "arc lights" coming from the ground itself. Each time they approached the areas, the lights would stop.

On another occasion Crystall was in a field with two other people when a strong blast of warm air came from below, *through* the ground. She located additional residents who heard drilling noises at night and found evidence of strange digging on their property.

Using all this information she did some research and discovered an amazing fact: Orange County in upstate New York (which includes Pine Bush) is one of the few locations on earth to find several rare metals including beryllium, zirconium and titanium. Interestingly, all three ores are used in nuclear engineering. Crystall speculated that the UFOs were not only mining these metals, but were constructing underground bases.

During this time, one of the biggest UFO waves in United State's history was sweeping across the Hudson Valley area of upstate New York. Low flying triangular-shaped craft flying low over homes and highways were generating thousands of reports, inundating police stations in several counties with calls. The Pine Bush phenomenon had gone state-wide.

The reports caught the attention of researcher Philip Imbrogno who became the premier documenter of the wave, eventually co-

201

writing a book, *The Hudson Valley UFOs,* and other follow-up books. As he began to catalogue the sightings, he, like Crystall, wondered why this area was experiencing such high levels of activity.

Looking for patterns, he quickly noticed what appeared to be a higher number of sightings over the areas known for mining. At one point during his investigation, he was contacted by a man who claimed to be a CIA agent. The agent told them that the aliens have, in fact, established several underground bases in the area, including in Orange, Putnam and Ulster Counties.

Also consider the following letter which was published in July 1984 in the *New York Post*: "Why are people seeing all these UFOs all of a sudden in the Hudson River Valley area? The answer is simple: there seems to be some kind of underground activity in the Brewster area in the old abandoned iron ore mines. Some years ago the government went out of its way to purchase the land that the mines are located on and people who live in the area, including myself, have seen military vehicles entering the dirt roads. They never come out."

The writer goes on to describe UFO sightings, helicopter encounters, hearing strange noises at night and more. He speculates that the government or the aliens have "established an underground base in which some type of experimental aircraft is being kept."

Learning of this information Imbrogno confirmed that in 1967 the government did, in fact, purchase property around the mines in Brewster and nearby Putnam Valley and Lake Carmel.

Regarding the Pine Bush area, Imbrogno has come to the same conclusions as Crystall that aliens are both mining rare metals and building underground bases.

Spring Creek Mine

Located in Spring Creek Ridge in the Sellway wilderness outside of Twin Falls, Idaho, the Spring Creek Mine became the target of a bizarre UFO-mine encounter.

The case was investigated by pioneering researchers Coral and Jim Lorenzen. The witness, Mr. Buzz Montague, had read one of their books and after experiencing his encounter, contacted them to report his case.

Mr. Montague often hunted in the area of the Spring Creek Mines and had observed strange activity there on multiple occasions throughout the 1960s. The incident that prompted him to write to the Lorenzens occurred in the company of his friend William Andrews sometime in 1965 (exact date not given.)

The two men were camped on a bluff overlooking the valley where the mine was located. Waking early in the morning they saw a strange silver object low in the sky over the ore dump, where all the waste matter from the mine was dumped. Observing it through the 10-power scopes attached to their rifles, they realized it was only one of four objects, each of which hovered directly over the ore dump. Above these four was a larger cigar-shaped craft complete with portholes. All were totally silent.

According to the report on the case: "Protruding from the top of the objects were four hose-like devices which were inserted into the slag piles and were moving around. After a period of time, one by one, the objects elevated and ascended into the air; at this time, the large object hovering at about 1,000 feet above the terrain, was spotted. An elongated, cigar-shaped object, it had four depressions on its underside. When the small objects reached the object, they fitted themselves into the depressions after which there was no indication that there had been a depression there to begin with. After another short period of time, the objects detached themselves from the cigar-shaped craft and returned to the slag heap."

The two men watched the objects for more than an hour as they made no less than four trips from the slag-heap back up to the larger cigar-shaped craft. Finally, all four craft returned to the large one, which moved to the northwest, upward and out of sight.

What makes this case interesting is that the UFOs were studying discarded material from which all useful ores had been extracted. If ETs were truly intent on mining, then why exhibit so much interest in slag heaps? Researchers have raised the possibility that they might have been attempting to determine the type of ore which had been removed, or the methods used.

French Gulch Gold Mine

For most people, seeing a UFO is a once-in-a-lifetime experience. For others, however, it is a regular part of life. A good example is Clint and Jane Chapin (pseudonyms) of the small town of French Gulch in northern California. The Chapins reside in a trailer in a remote area. They make their living from their gold mine located on their property. The French Gulch case is particularly interesting because it involves considerable physical evidence.

The first of several encounters occurred on October 30, 1969 at 10:30 AM. The Chapins were outside their home when they observed a silvery oval-shaped object the size of a small car landed among the trees. Seconds later, the object lifted up, hovered briefly and then accelerated away.

The Chapins checked the area where the object had landed and found a strange pile of sand and metal. Realizing it might be valuable, they collected and stored the material in a safe place.

Their next encounter would occur seven years later. On December 27, 1976 at 11:00 AM, the Chapins (now in their seventies) were driving along the road near their home when they came across a patch of ice. Clint exited the truck and walked ahead to investigate the size of the ice patch. Just around the corner of the road, he observed a car-sized object the shape of half an egg, landed on the road ahead of him. He shouted to his wife to bring the gun.

Jane jumped out of the truck and started to run.

At that moment several things happened. The object took off. Jane reports that she ran into an invisible and impassible barrier, fell to the ground and lost consciousness. Clint reports that his left arm was pinned behind his back and he was thrown to the side of the road where he lost consciousness. Both woke up about fifteen minutes later. Both had urinated in their pants. Both felt sick and cold.

Afterwards, Jane suffered from a strange buzzing noise in her head, deteriorating vision and pains in her arms and legs. Clint also felt unwell, and suffered from chronic pain in his left arm. Doctors were unable to diagnose Jane's condition and called it "old age nervousness."

The Chapins sought further help and were eventually put in contact with pioneering researcher Jacques Vallee, whose book "UFOs: Challenge to Science" was one of the first to take a scientific look at the subject. Vallee interviewed the witnesses and was able to obtain the mysterious "sand" which the Chapins had collected at the site of one of their encounters.

One year later the Chapins would experience another bizarre encounter involving medical injuries. It was October 13, 1977. The couple was working at their gold mine when both felt a sudden wave of heat. Both instantly became ill, exhibiting symptoms similar to radiation sickness, including vomiting violently. While they didn't see any actual object or entity, they both feel that the experience is related to the UFO that had been harassing them around their mine. Following this incident, Clint's health deteriorated dramatically. He felt constantly weak, experienced heart trouble, and as Jane says, "Clint sweats when sitting on a chair, and at night he turns real red in the face."

On January 14, 1978 Jane finally encountered the occupant of the UFO that had been harassing her and her husband as they worked on their privately owned gold mine. The encounter occurred inside their trailer when Jane saw a figure suddenly appear. According to investigator Jacques Vallee, "The head was flat, with large eyes and a big nose."

One month later, in August, another witness corroborated the Chapin's story. An anonymous twelve-year-old boy, the son of a local doctor, observed an "unusual humanoid creature" near the area of the mine. The boy was reportedly "deeply upset" by the encounter.

A few months later on April 4, 1980, the Chapins would have their final and most dramatic encounter. Now in their mid-eighties, they were examining a road that had been cut through their property. Says Jane Chapin, "We turned to go down the road, and there was a skinny *thing* in the road...He was four-foot tall and skinny, maybe ninety pounds...and his egg [the UFO] was not 25 feet from us...He [the humanoid] took four steps toward us and my hand fell on my gun, and he turned around and walked back. He was in a gray suit, and he left no prints or prints of the egg. Clint could not move either...the thing vanished, then the egg went up in the air and turned west."

Two months later, Clint died of an apparent heart attack. To date Jane Chapin has experienced no further encounters.

Vallee had the "sand" collected by the Chapins analyzed in a scientific laboratory. The results were puzzling to say the least. While the material was composed of substances that are found on Earth, there were several inexplicable and unusual properties.

The analysts told Vallee, "The problem with your sand is that it's not sand...Perhaps it looks like sand to you, but it's not alluvial sand or stream sand or beach sand or mine-tailing sand or any kind of naturally formed sand...Here is some siltstone. Here is volcanic material; here, sulfide-bearing rock; green crystals; feldspar or porcelain; pyrite cubes. No quartz and no mica. All the fragments are very angular. All the components are common, but they don't belong together. This is a composite of rock fragments and manufactured materials...It's as if somebody had taken minerals from very different areas and had ground them together until it looked like sand."

Vallee offers no theory as to why the UFO deposited this material or what it means. However, he was particularly impressed by the Chapins' story and calls it his "favorite case."

He writes: "The Chapins, I was convinced, were not lying...I did believe them, and I still do."

Karnes City Uranium Mine

Late one evening in the summer of 1971, Conoco Oil Company employee Michael Harvey was working the night shift at the 85-acre open pit uranium mine located west of Karnes City, Texas. He and a half-dozen other employees were operating Caterpillar 657B earth movers and had reached a depth of 210 feet when suddenly, says Harvey, the entire pit "lit up as if it was daylight."

Harvey and all the other workers immediately stopped working and looked up to see a massive blinding white light directly over the mine. Says Harvey, "The light was so bright that I had to squint because it hurt my eyes. I remember hearing a high-pitched hissing noise and the hair on my arms stood on end. I was so scared, I fell to the ground and started praying."

The light was too bright to look at. The workers were frozen in fear for a few minutes until suddenly, the lights began to dim. Only then could Harvey and the other workers see the source of the light. "What I saw amazed me," said Harvey. "The object was round and the bright light was coming from the center of the bottom of the UFO. Around the perimeter of the craft were hundreds of penlight size light beams that alternated in all colors of the spectrum."

Harvey was struck by the beams' similarity to lasers. As he and the others watched, the object rose slowly upward for about ten seconds, then darted straight up and disappeared.

Harvey and his co-workers were deeply traumatized by the incident. "I was crying and shaking," said Harvey, "and so was everyone else."

When the next shift of workers arrived, Harvey and the others told them what they had seen. The new shift was skeptical and ridiculed the witnesses mercilessly. "But we got the last laugh," said Harvey. "This is how we proved it actually happened."

Says Harvey: "There is a vein of uranium ore that runs from George West Texas to almost

Texarkana Texas. When determining where to place a mine, the following steps are accomplished: (1) A geologist with a Geiger-counter flies over the area and finds the highest radiation reading. (2) Drilling trucks are sent out and core samples are drilled to determine the highest concentration of uranium ore. These core samples are drilled in a grid pattern and every core sample is given a tracking number and logged in showing the concentration and amount of uranium present. (3) The open pit mine is then laid out according to these core samples.

"When this UFO incident happened, we were about two feet away from a layer of hard rock called the 'tap rock' that lied directly on top of the uranium ore. The uranium ore varied in depth from 6 to 18 inches and had about the same brown color as low grade coal. Two days after this incident, the tap rock was removed to expose the uranium ore. We were astounded to find that the uranium ore was now a chalky white substance that had no radioactivity at all! There was a 250-foot diameter circle of this chalky material in the center of the pit. Outside of the circle, the uranium ore was still as potent as before the incident. Core samples don't lie. This chalky material was uranium before this incident."

In this case, there seems to be little doubt that the mine was the target of attention. Writes Harvey, "Many a night I have laid in my bed thinking about what happened. I think the UFO needed the uranium for some reason."

Other similar cases could be cited, but by now, the mine-UFO connection should be obvious. Corroborating these reports are the scores of accounts of ETs exiting their craft with little shovels and digging small holes in the surrounding soil.

As these cases show, some UFO occupants are apparently geologists conducting multiple mining operations. The fact that UFOs visit these locations on repeated occasions reveals not only their strong interest in mines, but also that they are actively engaged in some type of agenda that involves these mines.

Another unique feature of UFO-mine encounters are those cases involving physical evidence. While many cases rely solely on eyewitness testimony, several cases involved physical evidence that is difficult to explain by conventional means.

Take the case of amateur prospector Stephen Michalak. On May 20, 1967, Michalak was prospecting for gold in the Falcon Lake area in Manitoba, Canada when a UFO landed next to him. He approached the object, which took off, blasting Michalak with heat and setting his shirt on fire.

Michalak immediately became ill, suffering a headache and vomiting. He went straight to the hospital where he suffered dizziness, nausea, hives, diarrhea, weakness, numbness, swelling of joins and hands, a burning sensation on his neck and chest, eye irritation and fainting. He was unable to keep any food down and over the next few weeks lost twenty-two pounds. His blood lymphocyte level dropped from a normal twenty-five to an alarming sixteen percent. He was examined by more than twenty-seven doctors, and the only diagnosis that seemed to fit was exposure to radiation.

Equally baffling were the findings at the landing site. Stewart Hunt of the Department of Health and Social Welfare investigated the area and found that it showed "significant" levels of radium 226, which could not be produced naturally.

Later Michalak returned to the site with a friend and found two strange "W-shaped" silver bars and chunks of silver exactly where the object had hovered. Researcher Brian Cannon analyzed the silver and found that the silver concentration was "much higher than normally would be found in native silver such as sterling or coinage." Also, the metal showed signs of heating, bending and radioactivity. Finally, the sample was imbedded on the outside with fine quartz crystals and small crystals of a uranium silicate material and pitchblende, and feldspar and hematite.

Not surprisingly, the case caused considerable controversy and for many years was covered up by the Canadian government. Even today, the full files on the case have not been released. Of most interest here are the strange effects on the silver ore. Once again, we have a UFO hovering over a mining area and causing unexplained changes in the ground beneath it.

Not only do these types of cases provide compelling evidence of UFO reality, they also have the potential to reveal how UFOs might use their technology to extract geological materials, and what types of materials they might be interested in. Finally, it is likely that mines are disproportionally more likely to be visited by UFOs than another mundane area. Therefore, a UFO stake-out of mines might have potential to allow for repeated predicted observations of UFOs engaged in low level activity, which would be the perfect opportunity for cutting edge live fieldwork.

Take the recent events in the Daivik Diamond Mine located in the Canadian Arctic. In September 2012, mine workers allegedly observed a massive lenticular-shaped object which hovered above the mine and sent down several beams of light. According to researcher, Scott C. Waring, numerous employees in the mine rushed out to observe the object and the beams of light. One worker took several photographs, which appear to show a large disk-like object with multiple shafts of light emitted from the center. An analysis of the photo also shows what appear to be three additional objects. According to Waring, authorities at the mine attempted to cover-up the sighting.

Waring is skeptical that the aliens have any interest in the mine for its materials. Writes Waring, "I don't believe aliens have an interest in diamonds, however, it is possible there is another material they are interested in nearby. Also the arctic ocean area would be a great location for an underwater base entrance."

As bizarre as this all sounds, many researchers have come to similar conclusions.

As an end-note, consider the following unsubstantiated case, which took place on August 27, 1989 in Donetsk, Ukraine, in Russia.

An electrical worker in a mine more than 350 feet below the surface saw "two strangers" standing by the electric train depot. Knowing that nobody else was supposed to be there and feeling a strange fear, the witness hid and observed the figures, watching them as they studied various types of equipment. Finally he began to walk forward, asking them, "Who are you? What are you doing here?"

The figures stopped moving and looked at him. As he approached them, the mine-worker suddenly realized they were not human. According to the report: "They were short creatures, dwarf-like, with sallow facial complexions, and features he could not recognize as human. Both were dressed in silvery-colored coveralls and on their chest they had lighted circles and luminous dots circling around, like the screen of an oscillograph. After standing for a while, the entities turned around and walked away, quickly moving away, floating just above the ground. In several seconds they vanished behind a bend in the underground tunnel."

Extraterrestrial miners? Stranger things have happened.

BEHIND THE SCENES: "Mining Data on UFOs" was originally titled: "UFOs and Mines." It appeared in "Perihelion Magazine" (February 2014 issue) after the editor wisely changed the title. This was an article I had always intended to write, but somehow just never got around to it. Then to my delight, the editor at Perihelion heard about my research and asked if I would contribute an article. He asked me to focus on the scientific aspects of UFOs, as his reader base is scientifically oriented. I hope I succeeded in that regard. As with many of the other articles, I updated it and added a few new cases. As far as I know, this is the first comprehensive collection and analysis of UFO-mine encounters.

Epilogue

I hope you have enjoyed this book. We have explored a wide variety of topics and ventured into areas not often explored. One of the questions I hear most is, "Why are the aliens here?" As this book has shown, aliens are here for many different reasons, and the alien agenda is wide and varied.

In some cases, UFOs are clearly interested in our minerals; in others our DNA seems to be the target. Sometimes they are here to collect animals or plants; sometimes they just want to talk. And sometimes, they like to dress up as clowns!

As we have seen, if you see a UFO, it's probably not a good idea to shoot at it, and you might consider the possibility that some of these UFOs are being piloted not by aliens, but by humans. Equally, it might be wise to consider the possibility that some of the human-looking people we see on the street are not from here, and are actually aliens in disguise, walking among us. Yes, there's definitely much more to the UFO phenomenon than first meets the eye.

If you enjoyed this volume, you might also enjoy the other forthcoming future volumes in this series. For more information about the author and his books, please visit his website at: www.prestondennett.weebly.com

Sources

Chapter One: Conversations with Extraterrestrials

The information in this chapter was obtained through personal interviews with UFO witnesses and the author.

Chapter Two: Phone Call from an Alien

Cameron, Grant. *Alien Bedtime Stories.* It's All Connected Publishing, 2015, 268-271. www.presidentialufo.com

Dennett, Preston. *One in Forty: The UFO Epidemic.* Commack, NY: Kroshka Books, 1997, pp221-256.

Fowler, Raymond. *The Watchers.* New York: Bantam Books, 1990, pp129-140.

Hopkins, Budd. *Intruders: The Incredible Visitation at Copley Woods.* New York: Random House, 1987, pp19-20.

Keel, John. *The Mothman Prophecies.* New York: Tor Books, 1991, pp107-109.

Keyhoe, Major Donald E. *Aliens from Space: The Real Story of Unidentified Flying Objects.* New York: New American Library, 1973, p56.

Mishlove Ph.D., Jeffrey. *The PK Man: A True Story of Mind Over Matter.* Charlottesville, VA: Hampton Roads Publishing Company, Inc., pp23-24.

Stevens, Wendelle C. *UFO...Contact From the Pleiades: A Supplementary Investigation Report.* Tucson, AZ: UFO Photo Archives, 1983, pp508-509.

Strieber, Whitley. *Communion: A True Story.* New York: William Morrow & Company, 1987. pp139-140.

Van Vlierden, Karl and Lt. Col. Wendelle C. Stevens (ret.). *UFO Contact from Planet Koldas: A Cosmic Dialogue.* Tucson, AZ: UFO Photo Archives, 1986, pp9-12, 21-30, 297.

Wilkins, Harold. *Flying Saucers Uncensored.* New York: Pyramid Books, 1955, p75.

Chapter Three: UFO: Don't Shoot!

Edward, Frank. *Flying Saucers – Serious Business.* Secaucus, NJ: Citadel Press, 1966, pp32-33.

Fowler, Raymond E. *UFOs: Interplanetary Visitors.* Englewood Cliffs, NJ: Prentice-Hall, Inc., 1974, p264-265.

Good, Timothy. *Above Top Secret.* New York: William Morrow & Co., 1993, pp15-17.

Green, Gabriel & Warren Smith. *Let's Face the Facts about Flying Saucers.* New York: Popular Library, 1967, pp89-90.

Haines, Ph.D., Richard F. *CE-5: Close Encounters of the Fifth Kind.* Naperville, IL: Sourcebooks, 1999, p217.

Jarvis, Sharon (Editor.) *The Uninvited: True Tales of the Unknown, Vol. II.* New York: Bantam Books, 1989, pp155-176.

Lorenzen, Coral & Jim. *Flying Saucer Occupants.* New York: Signet Books, pp99-100, 122-123.

Lorenzen, Jim & Coral. *UFOs over the Americas.* New York: Signet Library, 1968, p46.

Machlin, Milt (Editor.) *The Total UFO Story.* New York: Dale Books, 1979, p247.

Silverman, Dwight. "Woman Tells of Too-Close Encounter With Aliens." *Chronicle.* Houston, TX, March 1989.

Steiger, Brad. *Alien Meetings.* New York: Ace Books, 1978, pp145-146.

Stringfield, Leonard H. *Situation Red: The UFO Siege.* New York: Fawcett Crest Books, 1977, pp85-86, 163-164.

Torres, Noe and Ruben Uriarte. *Aliens in the Forest: The Cisco Grove UFO Encounter.* Edinburg, TX: RoswellBooks.com, 2011.

https://www.4shared.com/mp3/Wb0P-vvqba/ClovisNM_Interview.html

Chapter Four: Alien Zoos

Clarke, Ardy Sixkiller. *Sky People: Untold Stories of Alien Encounters in Mesoamerica.* Pompton Plains, NJ: New Page Books, 2015, pp255-258

Fowler, Raymond E. *The Andreasson Affair: The Amazing Documented Account of One Woman's Terrifying Encounter With Alien Beings.* New York: Bantam Books, l979, pp5l-72.

----. *The Andreasson Affair: Phase Two - The Continuing Investigation of A Woman's Abduction By Alien Beings.* Englewood Cliffs, NJ: Prentice-Hall, Inc., l982, pp94-124.

----. *The Watchers: The Secret Design behind UFO Abduction.* New York: Bantam Books, 1990, pp96-103, 202-203, 213.

Lorenzen, Coral and Jim. *Encounters with UFO Occupants.* New York: Berkley Publishing Corp, l976, pp227-230.

Mack, John E., MD. *Abduction: Human Encounters with Aliens.* New York: Charles Scribner's Sons, l994, ppl57-158.

Turner Ph.D., Karla. *Into The Fringe: A True Story of Alien Abduction*. New York: Berkley Books, 1992, pp161-169.

~ Twiggs, Denise Rieb and Bert Twiggs. *Secret Vows: Our Life with Extraterrestrials*. Tigard, OR: Wild Flower Press, l992, ppl68, 187.

~ Wilson, Katharina. *The Alien Jigsaw*. Portland, OR: Puzzle Publishing, 1993, pp55-58, 116-117.

Chapter Five: UFOs over Graveyards

Corrales, Scott. "Strange Places: UFOs and Cemeteries." *Fate*. Lakeville, MN: Fate Magazine, Inc., Vol. 54, #10, Issue 619, October 2001, pp14-148.

Editors. "Paperboy Reports Close Sighting in Nova Scotia Cemetery." *MUFON UFO Journal*. Seguin, TX: Mutual UFO Network, June 2000, #286, p13.

Fowler, Raymond. *Casebook of a UFO Investigator*. Englewood Cliffs, NJ: Prentice-Hall, 1981, pp26-27.

----. *UFOs: Interplanetary Visitors*. New York: Bantam Books, 1974, pp22-23, 216, 319.

Hynek, J. Allen. *The UFO Experience: A Scientific Inquiry*. New York: Ballantine Books, 1972, p139.

Lorenzen, Jim & Coral. *UFOs over the Americas*. New York: Signet Books, 1968, pp160-162.

Lorenzen, Coral & Jim. *UFOs: The Whole Story*. New York: Signet Books, 1969, pp159-160.

Redfern, Nicholas. *The FBI Files: The FBI's UFO Top Secrets Exposed*. New York: Simon Schuster, 1998, p196.

Teets, Bob. *West Virginia UFOs: Close Encounters in the Mountain State*. Terra Alta, WV: Headline Books, 1995, p196.

Vallee, Jacques. *Passport to Magonia*. Chicago, IL: Contemporary Books, 1969, 1993, p222.

Walden Ed.D., James L. *The Ultimate Alien Agenda: The Re-Engineering of Humankind*. St Paul, MN: Llewellyn Publications, 1998, pp26-46, 170-171.

www.mufon.com
www.ufocasebook.com

Chapter Six: They Walk Among Us

Beckley, Timothy Green. *Strange Encounters*. New Brunswick, NJ: Inner Light Publications, 1992, pp51-52.

Bryan, C.D.B. *Close Encounters of the Fourth Kind: Alien Abduction, UFOs and the Conference at M.I.T.* New York: Alfred A. Knopf, 1995, pp334-338.

Conroy, Ed. *Report on Communion*. New York: Avon Books, 1989, pp18-20.

Good, Timothy. *Alien Base: The Evidence for the Extraterrestrial Colonization of Earth*. New York: Avon Books, 1998, pp153-154.

Holzer, Hans. *The UFOnauts*. Greenwich, CT: Fawcett Publications, pp213-238.

Hopkins, Budd. *Intruders: the Incredible Visitations at Copley Woods*. New York: Random House, 1987, 90-98.

Jacobs Ph.D., David. *The Threat*. New York: Simon & Schuster. 1998, 185-188, 190-197, 251, 255-257.

Jordan, Debbie and Kathie Mitchell. *Abducted: the Story of Intruders Continues*. New York: Dell Books, 1995, 46-47.

Salter Jr. John R. "An Account of the Salter UFO Encounters of March 1988." JRS' May 1992 paper present at the *International Symposium of UFO Research*. (Int'l Assoc. for New Science, Denver, 1989, p4.)

Strieber, Whitley. *Transformation: The Breakthrough*. New York: Beech Tree Books, 1988, 223.

Strieber, Whitley and Ann Strieber (Editors.) *The Communion Letters*. New York: Harper-Prism, 1997, pp196-197, 206-207.

Walters, Ed and Frances Walters. *UFO Abductions in Gulf Breeze*. New York: Avon Books, 1999, pp273-274.

www.nuforc.org

Chapter Seven: The Alien-Clown Connection

Bryan, C. D. B. *Alien Abduction: UFOs and the Conference at MIT*. New York: Alfred A Knopf, 1995, pp216-221.

Collings, Beth an Anna Jamerson. *Connections: Solving Our Alien Abduction Mystery*. Newberg, OR: Wild Flower Press, 1996, pp38-39-46, 108.

Fowler, Raymond E. *The Andreasson Legacy*. New York: Marlowe and Company, 1997, pp259-336, 345.

Hopkins, Budd. *Witnessed*. New York: Pocket Books, 1996, pp356-398.

Horn, Wesley. "The Alien in the Cowboy Hat." *Fate*. Lakeville, MN: Fate Magazine, Inc., Jan 1998.

Strieber, Whitley. *Communion*. New York: William Morrow & Company, 1987, pp72-175.

Strieber, Whitley. *Transformation: The Breakthrough*. New York: Beech Tree Books, 1988, p150, 206.

Strieber, Whitley, and Anne Strieber. (Editors.) *The Communion Letters*. New York: Harper-Prism, 1997, p263.

Chapter Eight: The Intimidation & Murder of UFO Witnesses.

Butler, Brenda; Dot Street; Jenny Randles. *Sky Crash: A Cosmic Conspiracy*. London: Grafton Books, 1984, pp43-46.

Flammonde, Paris. *UFOs Exist*! New York: Ballantine Books, 1976, pp15-126.

Gordon, Danny B. & Paul Dellinger. *Don't Look Up! The Real Story Behind the Virginia Sightings*. Madison, NC: Empire Publishing, 1988, pp73-74, 134-139, 187.

Randle, Kevin D. *A History of UFO Crashes*. New York: Avon Books, 1995, pp8-27.

Randle, Kevin D. & Donald Schmitt. *The Truth about the UFO Crash at Roswell*. New York: M. Evans & Company, Inc., 1994, pp72-76.

Randles, Jenny. *From Out of the Blue*. New York: Berkley Books, 1991, 1993, ppVII-IX, 74-75, 105-106, 109-110.

Steinman, William S. *UFO Crash at Aztec: a Well-Kept Secret*. Tucson, AZ: UFO Photo Archives, 1986, pp393-401.

Turner Ph.D., Karla. *Taken: Inside the Alien-Human Agenda*. Roland, AR: Kelt Works, 1994, pp151-179.

Chapter Nine: Project Redlight

Cooper, Milton William. "Classified Above Top Secret." *UFO Universe*. New York: Condor Books, Fall 1989.

Dennett, Preston. *One in Forty: The UFO Epidemic*. Commack, NY: Kroshka Books, 1996.

Dennett, Preston. (Personal files.)

Hamilton, Will. "The Military's Secret Space Program." *UFO*. Los Angeles, CA: California UFO, Vol. 3, No #4.

http://www.examiner.com/article/indiana-cemetery-ufo-may-be-classified-air-force-project.

Chapter Ten: Mining Data on UFOs

Adamski, George. *Inside the Spaceships*. Vista, CA: George Adamski Foundation, 1953, 1955 pp295-296.

Barker, Gray. *They Knew Too Much About Flying Saucers.* New York: University Books, 1956, pp36-58.

Bowen, Charles (Editor.) *The Humanoids: A Survey of Worldwide Reports of Landings of Unconventional Aerial Objects and Their Occupants.* Chicago, IL: Henry Regnery Company, 1969, pp146-147.

Corrales, Scott. "Argentina: UFO over the Gualcamayo Mine." *Inexplicita: The Journal of Hispanic Ufology.* January 10, 2009. http://inexplicata.blogspot.com/2009/01/argentina-ufo-over-gualcamayo-mine.html

Crystall, Ellen. *Silent Invasion: The Shocking Discoveries of a UFO Researcher.* New York: Paragon House, 1991, p86-92, 119.

Dolan, Richard M. *UFOs for the 21st Century Mind.* Rochester, NY: Richard Dolan Press, 2014, pp91-92.

Dongo, Tom. *The Alien Tide: The Mysteries of Sedona, Book Two*. Sedona, AZ: Hummingbird Publishing Co, 1990.

Good, Timothy. *Above Top Secret: the Worldwide UFO Cover-up*. New York: William Morrow & Company, pp195-200.

Hamilton, William F. *The Phoenix Lights Mystery*. Merrimack, NH: Write-to-Print, 2001.

Harvey, Michael. "Bizarre 1971 UFO Encounter Over Texas Uranium Mine." *UFO Evidence.Org*. http://www.ufoevidence.org/cases/case1070.htm

Imbrogno, Philip J. & Marianne Horrigan. *Contact of the 5th Kind*. St. Paul, MN: Llewellyn Publications, 1997, pp168, 181, 190, 216.

Lorenzen, Coral. *Flying Saucers: The Startling Evidence of the Invasion from Outer Space*. New York: Signet Books, 1966, pp17-18.

Lorenzen, Jim & Coral. "Idaho Mining UFOs." *APRO Bulletin*. Vol. 22, #2, (Sept/Oct 1973.) http://www.ufoevidence.org/cases/case300.htm

www.nuforc.com

Pfeifer, Ken. "Alien Encounter in a Deep Mine in Russia." http://worldufophotosandnews.org/?p=4007

Renzi, Steve. "MUFON." *Desert Leaf*. Tucson, AZ, Jul/Aug 2006. (See UFONS, Aug 2006, #445.)

Ropp, Thomas. "Forget Roswell; Arizona's UFO Hotbed." *Newsday*. Melville, NY, Jul 6, 1997.

Taylor, Ellis. "Meat and Feathers: A UFO Sighting over Paraburdoo in North-West Australia." http://ellisctaylor.homestead.com/sightingparaburdoo.html

Vallee, Jacques. *Dimensions: A Casebook of Alien Contact.* Chicago, IL: Contemporary Books, Inc., 1988, pp181-193.

Waring, Scott. "UFO over Diamond Mine in Arctic." http://www.ufosightingsdaily.com/2012/09/ufo-over-diamond-mine-in-arctic-sept.html

p 168. Leah MALEY

Other Books by Preston Dennett

UFOs over Arizona..................Schiffer Publishing, 2016
UFOs over Nevada..................Schiffer Publishing, 2014
UFOs over New Mexico...............Schiffer Publishing, 2012
Ghosts of Greater Los Angeles......Schiffer Publishing, 2010
Bigfoot, Yeti & Other Apemen.......Chelsea House, 2009
UFOs over New York.................Schiffer Publishing, 2008
Aliens & UFOs......................Chelsea House, 2008
The Coronado Island UFO Incident...Galde Press, 2007
Human Levitation...................Schiffer Publishing, 2007
Supernatural California............Schiffer Publishing, 2006
UFOs over California...............Schiffer Publishing, 2005
Out-of-Body Exploring..............Hampton Roads Publ., 2004
California Ghosts..................Schiffer Publishing, 2004
Extraterrestrial Visitations.......Llewellyn Publ., 2001
UFOs Over Topanga Canyon...........Llewellyn Publ., 1999
One in Forty: The UFO Epidemic....Kroshka Books, 1997
UFO Healings......................Wild Flower Press, 1996

ABOUT THE AUTHOR

Preston Dennett began investigating UFOs and the paranormal in 1986 when he discovered that his family, friends and co-workers were having dramatic unexplained encounters. Since then, he has interviewed hundreds of witnesses and investigated a wide variety of paranormal phenomena. He is a field investigator for the Mutual UFO Network (MUFON), a ghost hunter, a paranormal researcher, and the author of 18 books and more than 100 articles on UFOs and the paranormal. His articles have appeared in numerous magazines including *Fate, Atlantis Rising, MUFON UFO Journal, Nexus, Paranormal Magazine, UFO Magazine, Mysteries Magazine, Ufologist* and others. His writing has been translated into several different languages including German, French, Portuguese, and Icelandic. He has appeared on numerous radio and television programs, including *Coast-to-Coast* and the History Channel's *Deep Sea UFOs* and *UFO Hunters*. His research has been presented in the *LA Times,* the *LA Daily News,* the *Dallas Morning News* and other newspapers. He has taught classes on various paranormal subjects and lectures across the United States. He currently resides in southern California. www.prestondennett.weebly.com

ABOUT THE ARTIST:

Christine "Kesara" Dennett knew she would be an artist from an early age when she got in trouble for drawing dragons in grade school. A sculptor, bead-worker, illustrator, painter and more, Kesara has worked in countless mediums. Beginning in 1988, she began to produce illustrations about UFOs. Since then she has produced thousands of drawings of UFOs and aliens. She has worked closely with many experiencers and investigators to accurately portray UFOs and extraterrestrials. Her drawings have appeared in many magazines including UFO Universe, Unsolved Sightings, UFO Files, Encounters and more. She has illustrated several books about UFOs, and her artwork was also featured on the television series, "Roswell." Today she is a leading UFO artist and continues to work closely with people who are having extraterrestrial experiences. She resides in southern Oregon.

www.kesara.org

Printed in Great Britain
by Amazon